At Least A Thousand Things To Do

by
Cherrie Farnette
Imogene Forte
Barbara Loss

illustrated by Karen Kennedy

Library of Congress Catalog Number 77-83655
ISBN Number 0-913916-53-6

Copyright © 1977 by Incentive Publications. All rights reserved. Printed in Nashville, Tennessee, United States of America. No part of this publication may be reproduced, stored in a retrieval system, or transmitted, in any form or by any means, electronic, mechanical, photocopying, recording, or otherwise without prior written permission of Incentive Publications, except as noted below.

All pupil activity pages are designed to be used by individual pupils. Permission is hereby granted to the purchaser of one copy of AT LEAST A THOUSAND THINGS TO DO to reproduce copies of these pages in sufficient quantity for the pupils in one classroom.

AT LEAST A THOUSAND THINGS TO DO

A Career Awareness Activity Book

AT LEAST A THOUSAND THINGS TO DO is made up of reproducible pupil activity pages designed to help boys and girls develop awareness of the many facets of the work world, and to begin to explore and plan toward implementation of their own career options. A closer look at the work done by family members, neighbors and local citizens will lead to realization of more varying and complex career bases.

As various career roles and demands are considered, individual students will naturally begin to think in terms of their own career futures. It is at this point that strengths and weaknesses, interests, ambitions and personal preferences begin to be examined and sorted out. Within the context of exposure to the many facets of each career choice, realistic career expectancies may be well nurtured.

United States Office of Education Career Education guidelines have been embraced and incorporated. Thus, the scope of Career Education has been expanded to include the individual's life roles as citizen, family member and participant in aesthetic and recreational experiences. AT LEAST A THOUSAND THINGS TO DO includes activities related to each of the fifteen career clusters as designated by the USOE guidelines. The fifteen career clusters are:

1. Agri-Business and Natural Resources
2. Business and Office
3. Communication and Media
4. Construction
5. Consumer and Homemaking
6. Environment
7. Fine Arts and Humanities
8. Health Services
9. Hospitality, Recreation and Leisure
10. Manufacturing
11. Marine Science
12. Marketing and Distribution
13. Personal Services
14. Public Service
15. Transportation

The high interest/low vocabulary format has been maintained to encourage use of basic communication skills in the most positive and meaningful sense. The simple, easy-to-follow directions are self-explanatory and designed to encourage pupil independence. The Fringe Benefits accompanying many activities are presented to provide additional divergent thinking experiences. They may be used as optional free time activities or, in some instances, utilized as required follow-up assignments.

The reproducible pupil activity pages have been organized into four groups:

1. Surveying the Career Field
2. Exploring Career Options and Demands
3. Examining Human Interdependence
4. Looking to the Future

Each of the activities is designed to stand alone and to present one complete self-awareness experience. They may be used to supplement and reinforce adopted textbooks and courses of study, and are appropriate for use in either individual or group settings. While there is no need for a rigid sequence, each teacher will want to review the entire collection and plan the order and manner of presentation to meet the composite needs of his or her own group of students.

Cherrie Farnette
Imogene Forte
Barbara Loss

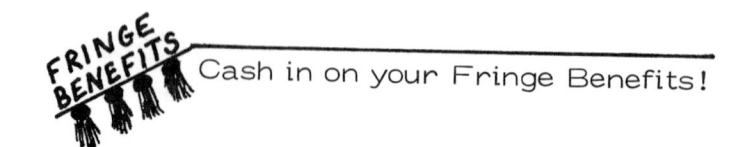

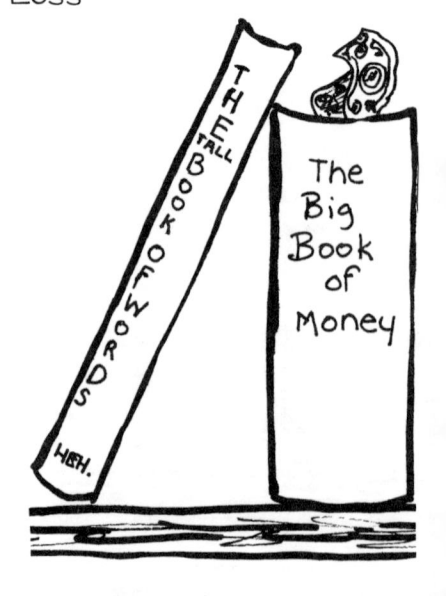

Cash in on your Fringe Benefits!

TABLE OF CONTENTS

I   Surveying the Career Field

         Family Career Tree...(career awareness)................. 9
         Occupational Directory...(defining occupations)............ 10
         Dependency Defined...(career roles)...................... 11
         Joint Accounts...(familiarity with occupations)............. 12
         Goods and Services...(goods and services production)...... 13
         Ad Comprehension...(job analysis)....................... 14
         Help Wanted!...(career awareness) 15
         Time Tally...(job demands)............................. 16
         Name That Job...(familiarity with occupations) 17
         Girls Can! Boys Can!...(career roles).................... 18
         Helping Hands...(job demands) 19
         Congratulations!...(workers and tools).................... 20
         She Can, He Can...(career possibilities).................. 21
         Compound Activities...(workers and tools)................. 22
         Pay Scale ...(defining terms)............................ 23
         Career ABC's...(career awareness) 24
         Telephonic Needs...(career awareness).... 25
         Instructor Information...(information sources)............. 26

II   Exploring Career Options and Demands

         Moving On...(transportation careers) 29
         Grow-Power...(environmental careers).................... 30
         Best Buys...(marketing and distribution careers).......... 31
         Writers' Workshop...(fine art and humanities careers)...... 32
         Directing Duties...(business and office careers)............ 33
         Sea Scape...(marine science careers) 34
         Special Delivery...(mail careers)......................... 35
         Consumer Guide...(consumer education)................... 36
         Making Tracks...(transportation careers) 37
         Natural Resource Scramble...(natural resource
           and agriculture occupations) 38
         Turnabout Teacher...(teaching careers) 39
         A Career Is Born...(career research)...................... 40
         Building Careers...(construction careers) 41
         Common Clusters...(career demands)..................... 42
         Oh Yes Girls Can!...(career options) 43
         Inter-Office Memo...(business and office careers).......... 44
         Beauty-Full Jobs...(personal service careers).............. 45
         Communication Exploration...(communications careers).... 46
         Paper Connections...(newspaper careers).................. 47
         Who Knows It?...(career demands) 48
         Device Dependence...(service careers).................... 49
         Move-Meant...(transportation careers) 50
         Scrambled Summers...(recreation careers)................. 51
         Try It...(advertising careers) 52
         Riddling Careers...(defining careers) 53
         Help Wanted...(job selection)............................ 54

	For Boys Too!...(career options)	55
	Hospital Hunt...(medical careers)	56
	Chore Check...(homemaking careers)	57
	Sport Pros...(sports careers)	58
	Job Counselor...(career counseling)	59
	Shops Galore...(consumer decision-making)	60
	Manufacturing Match...(manufacturing careers)	61
	Travel Talk...(recreation and leisure careers)	62
	Assembly Line...(production line activities)	63
	The Store...(marketing and distribution careers)	64
III	Examining Human Interdependence	
	Promises, Promises...(personal responsibilities)	67
	Predictable Casualties...(human interaction)	68
	Moving Connections...(career interdependence)	69
	Party Planning...(group interaction)	70
	Working Attitudes...(attitude appraisal)	71
	Message Mess-Up...(community interdependence)	72
	Monetary Connections...(human interdependence)	73
	Izzy Irresponsible?...(personal responsibility)	74
	Natural Forces...(career interdependence)	75
	Lending Lands...(international dependency)	76
	Puzzle Parts...(international dependency)	77
	World Wise...(world interdependence)	78
	Value Evaluation...(personal responsibility)	79
	Border Boundaries...(international dependency)	80
	Position Place...(group responsibility)	81
	Dependency File...(career dependence)	82
	Scrambled Needs...(human interdependence)	83
	Joint Decisions...(joint decision-making)	84
IV	Looking to the Future	
	Career Coat Of Arms...(goal setting)	87
	Goal To Go...(goal setting)	88
	Term Match...(career definitions)	89
	It's All In The "Name"...(career goals)	90
	Interview Inquiry...(job interviewing)	91
	Your Own Bag...(career investigation)	92
	Working Experiences...(volunteer work experience)	93
	Sign-N-Seal...(personal job references)	94
	Clothes Contact...(career planning)	95
	Application Blank...(job applications)	96
	Look Into The Future...(career predictions)	97
	Work Wanted...(job selection)	98
	Now And Then...(career prediction)	99
	Career Wheels...(career preparation)	100
	Future I.D....(career prediction)	101
	Elevation Exploration...(career opportunities)	102
	Time Span...(time scheduling)	103
	At Your Service...(job selection)	104
	Selected References	105

surveying the career field

NOTES

FAMILY CAREER TREE

Explore the occupations held by your family members. Complete the career tree by writing the appropriate jobs in the spaces below. Learn something new about each occupation before you list it.

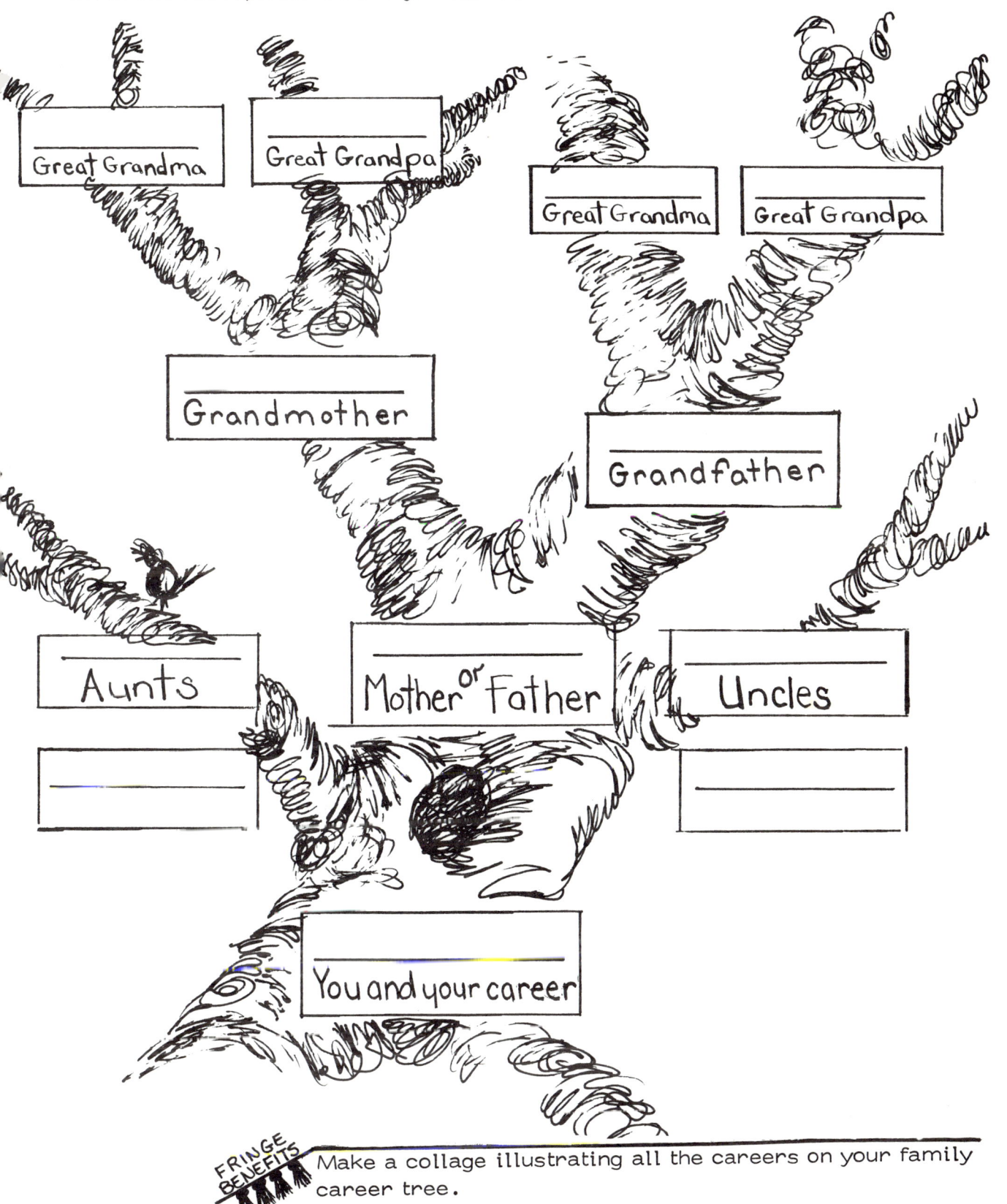

- Great Grandma
- Great Grandpa
- Great Grandma
- Great Grandpa
- Grandmother
- Grandfather
- Aunts
- Mother or Father
- Uncles
- You and your career

FRINGE BENEFITS Make a collage illustrating all the careers on your family career tree.

OCCUPATIONAL DICTIONARY

The occupations listed below may or may not be ones with which you are familiar. Use your dictionary as needed and write brief definitions for each one.

glazier _____

oiler _____

mason _____

stevedore _____

dispatcher _____

stenographer _____

actuary _____

mortician _____

astrologer _____

miller _____

horticulturist _____

mariner _____

oceanographer _____

philatelist _____

numismatist _____

draftsman _____

dietician _____

surveyor _____

Select one of the occupations above that really interests you and write a brief paragraph giving the personal qualifications and the kind of training necessary.

_____

_____

_____

DEPENDENCY DEFINED

To solve the puzzle and find the hidden word, read the sentences below. If the statement is true, color the numbered spaces as directed.

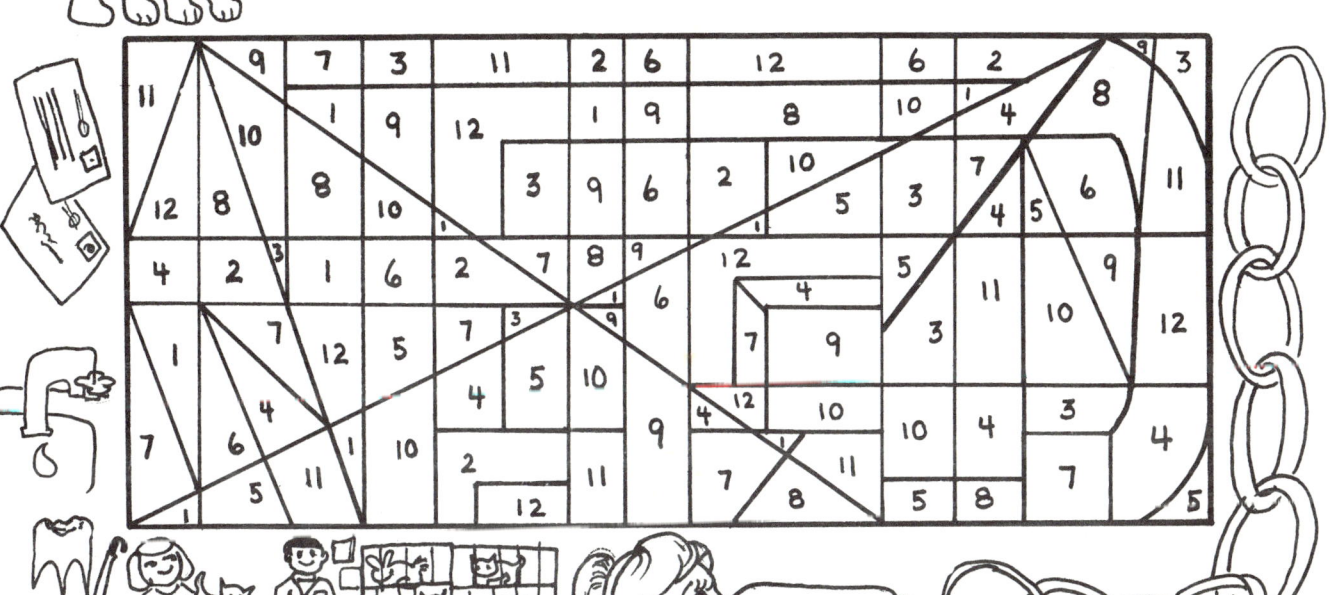

If we depend on veterinarians for the health of our pets, color the #1 spaces.
If we depend on plumbers to fix leaking faucets, color the #2 spaces.
If we depend on cosmetologists to design houses, color the #3 spaces.
If we depend on automobile mechanics to fix cars, color the #4 spaces.
If we depend on telephone operators to install phones, color the #5 spaces.
If we depend on butchers to prepare baked goods, color the #6 spaces.
If we depend on dentists for the care of our teeth, color the #7 spaces.
If we depend on bankers to provide savings accounts for our money, color the #8 spaces.
If we depend on police to deliver our mail, color the #9 spaces.
If we depend on electricians for our water supply, color the #10 spaces.
If we depend on librarians to help us find books, color the #11 spaces.
If we depend on sales clerks to help us find the goods we wish to buy, color the #12 spaces.

JOINT ACCOUNTS

Use this list of workers to fill in the missing "addends" in the account problems below.

clerk	photographer	butcher	roofer
electrician	cabinet maker	farmer	waiter
file clerk	draftsman	secretary	pupil

1. Baker
   + _____
   bread

2. Rancher
   + _____
   steak

3. Lumberjack
   + _____
   furniture

4. Model
   + _____
   picture

5. Principal
   Teacher
   + _____
   school

6. Cook
   Waitress
   + _____
   restaurant

7. Manager
   Stock person
   + _____
   department store

8. Construction worker
   Engineer
   + _____
   bridge

9. Executive
   + _____
   Receptionist
   Bookkeeper
   + _____
   office

10. Architect
    Carpenter
    + _____
    Plumber
    + _____
    house

FRINGE BENEFITS Choose one of the following products and make a list of necessary "addend" workers.

motion picture   automobile   hospital

GOODS AND SERVICES

Goods are products that are purchased. Services are things people do to earn money.

List three services that you can perform to earn money. (Example: mow the lawn)

_____

_____

_____

List five goods you are using today. (Example: pencil)

_____   _____

_____   _____

_____

List three services that you are receiving today. (Example: cooking)

_____   _____   _____

List three goods you would like to purchase and the place to go to purchase them.

Goods	Source
_____ -	_____
_____ -	_____
_____ -	_____

List three situations you have encountered (or will encounter) today that require both goods and services. List the goods and services.

Situation   Goods   Services

_____   _____   _____

_____   _____   _____

_____   _____   _____

AD COMPREHENSION

The Daily Sun May 21, 1979

EMPLOYMENT: part and full time.

★ Aggressive personality with telephone sales experience. Full or part-time for challenging position in sales and customer relations. Salary, incentives, benefits. Call Mrs. Soffy - 555-2222

MAN to learn drain cleaning and plumbing repair. Good driving record a must. Apply 2000 Wood Dr. - 688-6688.

OFFICE MANAGER, Accounting background, computer experience desirable. Aggressive take-charge person. Good work record. References. For industrial distributor Village area. 456-7899

YOUNG MAN needed, general auto service work. Please apply in person. April Tire Co., 8821 West.

CAREER in store management, high school grad. Some retail experience. $140 to $150. Ask for Tony Gray, Personnel. 993-4281.

PART-TIME Gas Station Attendant. Must be good at giving change. Apply in person. 10th St. & Smith Rd.

WAITRESS, female over 18. Days Mon. through Fri. Apply in person between 2:30 p.m. and 5 p.m. Mac's Restaurant, 2277 Frank Ave.

GUARDS WANTED: Male and female. All areas. Call anytime. 747-6655

UPHOLSTERER, experienced. Complete job. Part or full time. Good pay. 485-0115.

Interesting part-time reception work. 3 shifts, 9-1, 1-5, 5-9. $2.50 per hour plus bonus. 995-8884.

PROJECT ENGINEER: Engineer with at least 4 years experience in machine tool systems. Must be able to do both electrical and mechanical design. Graduate engineer preferred. Good pay and benefits. Apply at Phon Services, Inc., 3333 West Rd.

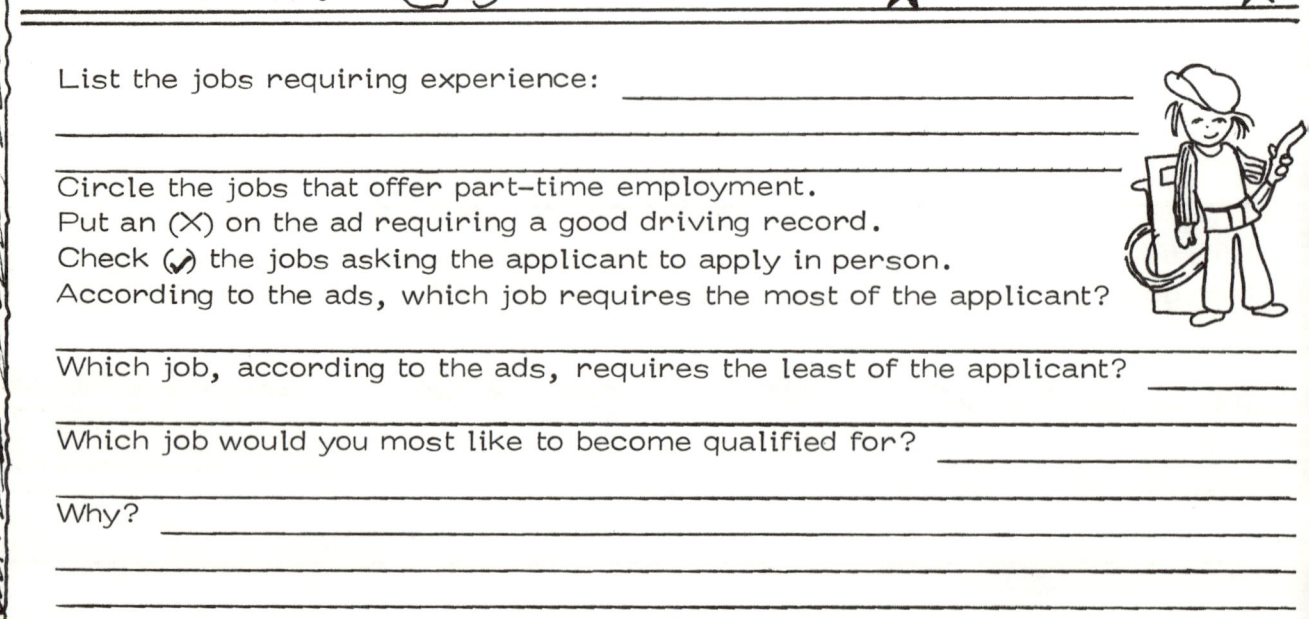

List the jobs requiring experience: _____
_____

Circle the jobs that offer part-time employment.
Put an (X) on the ad requiring a good driving record.
Check (✓) the jobs asking the applicant to apply in person.
According to the ads, which job requires the most of the applicant? _____

Which job, according to the ads, requires the least of the applicant? _____

Which job would you most like to become qualified for? _____

Why? _____
_____
_____

HELP WANTED!

What person would you call if you had these problems? List the names, occupations, addresses and telephone numbers for the problem solvers in the correct spaces.

1. You come home from school and you're tired, so you sit in your favorite wooden chair. It breaks into pieces! What person do you call for help?

   _____ _____ _____ _____
   Name   Occupation   Address   Phone

2. There's water in your basement! It begins to look like a flood. What person do you call for help?

   _____ _____
   Name   Occupation

   _____ _____
   Address   Phone

3. You smell gas! What person do you call for help?

   _____ _____ _____ _____
   Name   Occupation   Address   Phone

4. Your bicycle tire is flat. What person do you call for help?

   _____ _____ _____ _____
   Name   Occupation   Address   Phone

5. There is sound coming from your television set, but no picture appears on the screen. What person do you call for help?

   _____ _____ _____ _____
   Name   Occupation   Address   Phone

6. Your cat is sicker than a dog. What person do you call for help?

   _____ _____
   Name   Occupation

   _____ _____
   Address   Phone

15

TIME TALLY

Different jobs require different amounts of work time. Interview workers and ask the questions on this Time Tally Interview Sheet. Record their answers in the spaces provided.

✳ Workers Interviewed

	name: occupation:	name: occupation:	name: occupation:	name: occupation:
How many days a week do you work?				
How many hours do you work each day?				
How long is your lunch break?				
If you have other break times each day, how long are they?				
How many vacation days do you have each year?				

Answer these questions about <u>your</u> working time expectations. From the information gathered on the Interview Sheet, find the job that best matches your own career desires.

1. How many days a week do you expect to work? _____
2. How many hours a day do you expect to work? _____
3. How long do you expect to have for lunch break? _____
4. How long do you expect to have for other breaks during the day? _____
5. How many vacation days do you expect to get each year? _____

The jobs that match my time expectations are _____
_____

NAME THAT JOB

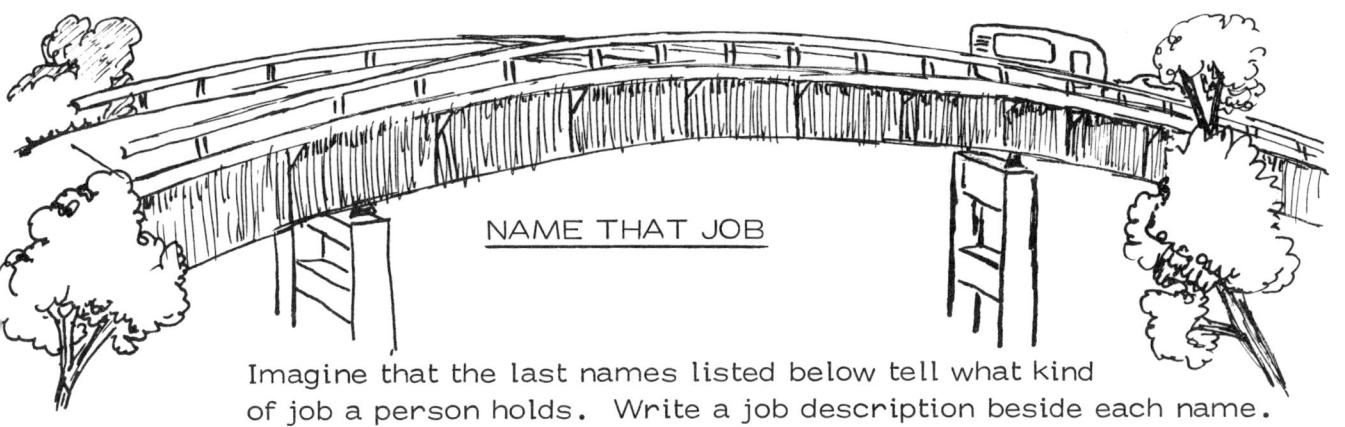

Imagine that the last names listed below tell what kind of job a person holds. Write a job description beside each name. (There may be more than one description for each name. Examples: Mr. Bridges is an engineer, or is a workman on the building of a bridge. Mrs. Gardner works on a farm and grows vegetables.)

Miller _____

Cook _____

Baker _____

Fisher _____

Taylor _____

Gardner _____

Mason _____

Butcher _____

Burns _____

Goldman _____

Glassman _____

Powers _____

Parker _____

Cutter _____

Waggoner _____

Barker _____

Pressman _____

GIRLS CAN! BOYS CAN!

Unscramble the letters to find the activities. Picture clues are given beside each scrambled word.

Boys can: e s w   _ _ _

k o c o   _ _ _ _

grow   l o f e r w s   grow _ _ _ _ _ _ _

s t i b y b a   _ _ _ _ _ _ _

Girls can:

collect   s c i t n e s   collect _ _ _ _ _ _ _

play   a b l l   play _ _ _ _

build   e f n e s c   build _ _ _ _ _ _

t n p i a   _ _ _ _ _ _

List the activities on the lines below. For each activity write the name of an occupation which requires the skills used in performing the activity.

Activity	Occupation
_____	_____
_____	_____
_____	_____
_____	_____
_____	_____
_____	_____
_____	_____
_____	_____

FRINGE BENEFITS Work with a friend. Make a list of four activities usually thought to be "girl" activities. Make a list of four activities usually thought to be "boy" activities. Discuss why the activities named can be enjoyed by boys <u>and</u> girls and their future occupations can be held by both men <u>and</u> women.

18

HELPING HANDS

Help solve each job problem below. Write the needed source of information in the numbered puzzle boxes.

ACROSS

1. Mike is offered a job overseas. He wants to know all about the country and its people. He could find this information in the _____.
4. Marge has one hour off for lunch. She must be prompt. She must watch the _____.
5. Sue travels in her work and must find the shortest route from one place to another. She needs a _____.
6. Chuck is a secretary and must correct all spelling errors. He needs a _____.
8. Dan is a chef and is asked to prepare a special dish. He could use a _____.

DOWN

2. June wants to find a new job in her town. She should look in the _____.
3. Lisa is a receptionist and is in charge of appointments. She will need a _____.
7. Jim is a fisherman and needs to know the weather conditions. He could get this information by listening to the _____.

FRINGE BENEFITS For each situation, identify another possible source of information.

19

CONGRATULATIONS!

These gifts have been sent to people who have just secured new jobs. Can you guess what type of jobs they have by the tools of trade included in the gift arrangements?

Write the job titles on the attached cards and state the reasons for your choices in the spaces provided.

Fringe Benefits — Add two arrangements for school jobs.

20

SHE CAN, HE CAN
===============

To solve the puzzle and find the hidden word, read the sentences below. If the statement is true, color the numbered puzzle spaces as directed.

If a girl can be a doctor, color the #1 spaces.
If a boy can be a nurse, color the #2 spaces.
If girls are smarter than boys, color the #3 spaces.
If boys are smarter than girls, color the #4 spaces.
If girls can be race car drivers, color the #5 spaces.
If boys can be cooks, color the #6 spaces.
If only girls can be dress designers, color the #7 spaces.
If only boys can be pilots, color the #8 spaces.
If girls can be what they want to be, color the #9 spaces.
If boys can be what they want to be, color the #10 spaces.

FRINGE BENEFITS Write a newspaper article telling why you think boys and girls should have equal chances to be what they want to be.

COMPOUND ACTIVITIES

Write a sentence using each of the compound words listed below. Make each sentence tell about a worker who would use the article.

Examples: (A) Mary and John had fun together at the <u>football</u> game because they were cheering for the same team.
(B) <u>Everytime</u> Joe and Jim get together they have a good time.

1. stepladder –

2. screwdriver –

3. chalkboard –

4. notebook –

5. dishpan –

6. washcloth –

7. ballpoint pen –

8. wastebasket –

9. wheelbarrow –

10. shoehorn –

FRINGE BENEFITS Use pastel chalk and colored paper to illustrate one of your sentences.

22

PAY SCALE

Use the dictionary. Find a term from the list given to match each definition below. Write the terms on the correct spaces to balance the scale. Use each term only once.

taxes   overtime   gross pay
income   net pay   deductions
benefits   salary   hourly wage

payment for work

contributions required by the government for support

work and pay for hours beyond regular job requirements

advantages offered to employee by employer

subtractions from pay or taxed income

a certain amount of money earned for each hour of work

what is remaining after all deductions are made

total earned before deductions are made

money received for labor or services; from the sale of property or from investments

FRINGE BENEFITS Work with a friend and your dictionary to find definitions for the following "money" terms: budget, expenses, withdrawal, deposit, checking account, savings account.

CAREER ABC'S

Write your own dictionary of careers. Identify interesting careers that begin with the letters of the alphabet and describe them.

Aa _____   Nn _____

Bb _____   Oo _____

Cc _____   Pp _____

Dd _____   Qq _____

Ee _____   Rr _____

Ff _____   Ss _____

Gg _____   Tt _____

Hh _____   Uu _____

Ii _____   Vv _____

Jj _____   Ww _____

Kk _____   Xx _____

Ll _____   Yy _____

Mm _____   Zz _____

FRINGE BENEFITS Draw a picture to go with each of your choices or select five careers and write a short essay about each.

TELEPHONIC NEEDS

Use the telephone directory to complete the following "mini directory" for your own use.

1. The name, station and number of a disc jockey I could call to play a record is _____.

2. The number I will call for the correct time is _____.

3. The number I could call when I need a temperature forecast is _____. I would talk with the _____.

4. The name, address and phone number of the best department store in town is _____
_____
_____

5. If I need to know a zip code I could call the _____ at this number.

6. To report a robbery I would call this number _____ and ask to speak with the _____.

7. If I need to find out about the fine for an overdue library book I would call this number _____ and ask for the _____.

Select one of the careers included in your "mini directory" and write its job description.

INSTRUCTOR INFORMATION

School Personnel

Science Teacher | Art Teacher | Music Teacher | Gym Teacher | Math Teacher | Industrial Arts Teacher
Home Ec. Teacher | Librarian | English Teacher | History Teacher | Language Teacher | Counselor

Use the School Personnel Listing above. Select the people you would go to in order to obtain the desired information.

1. You want to find a special book to read about the Civil War. Information source: _____

2. You want to learn to macramé. Information source: _____

3. You want to learn how to build a guitar. Information source: _____

4. You want to learn how to get stains out of your clothes. Information source: _____

5. You want to know more about job training possibilities. Information source: _____

6. You want to learn about Shakespeare. Information source: _____

7. You want to learn the rules of tennis. Information source: _____

8. You want to learn more about ecology. Information source: _____

9. You want to learn how to build a tree fort. Information source: _____

10. You want to redecorate your room. Information source: _____

11. You want to learn a new dance. Information source: _____

12. You want to learn to speak another language. Information source: _____

13. You want to learn the metric system. Information source: _____

exploring career options

NOTES

MOVING ON

Use these pictures to help you describe how transportation careers have changed through time. List the jobs in transportation for yesterday (the past), today (the present) and tomorrow (the future).

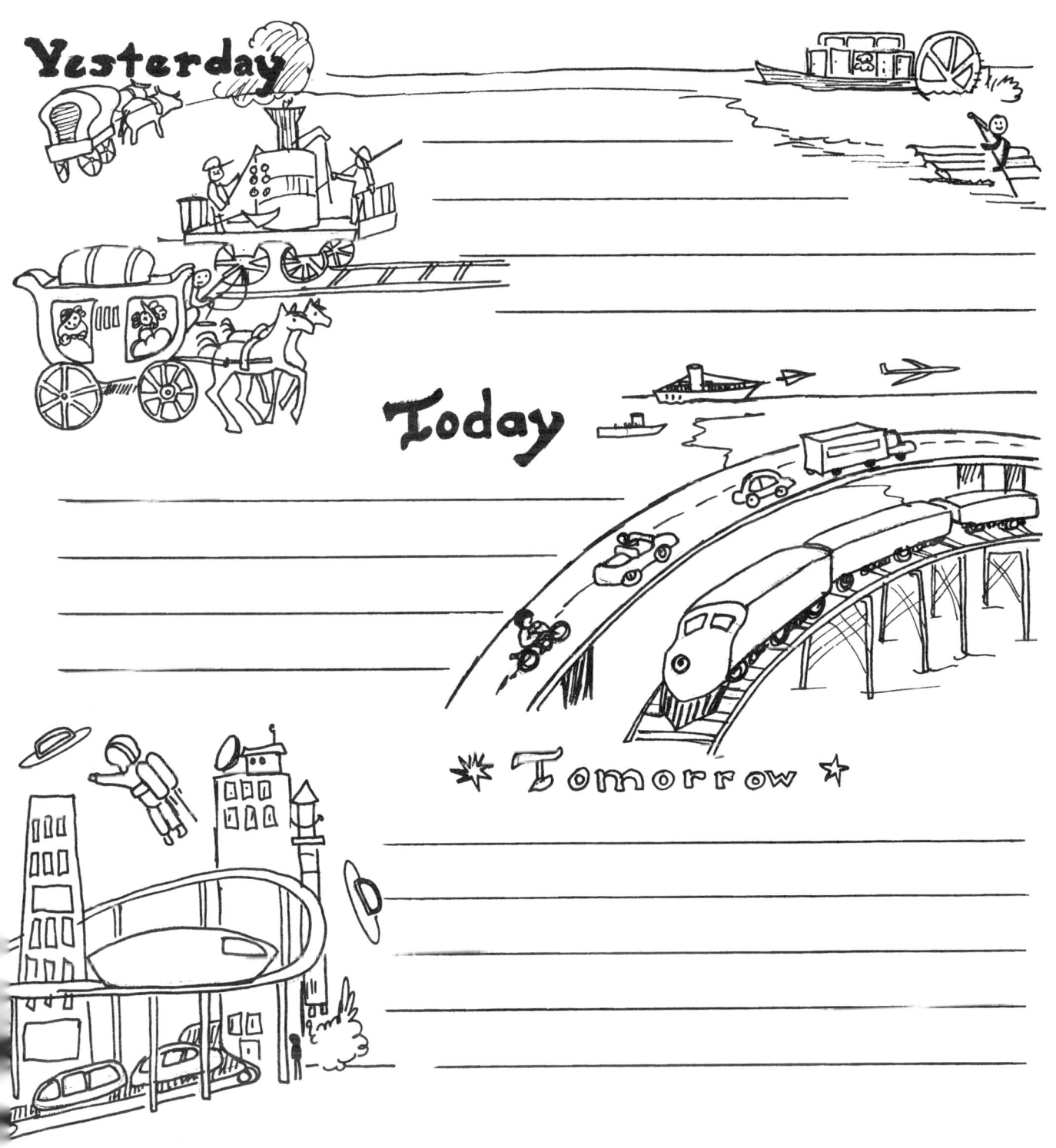

Yesterday
_____
_____
_____
_____
_____

Today
_____
_____
_____
_____
_____

Tomorrow
_____
_____
_____
_____
_____

List the new skills that will be needed by people in the transportation field in the future.

29

GROW-POWER

Many people today find that a mid-year career switch gives them a whole new "lease on life." It's not as uncommon as it once was for a doctor to decide to leave the medical profession at age fifty to become a minister, a teacher, a writer...for an accountant to turn to private business, and a homemaker to the law...or for a barber to become a tailor...

Describe mid-year career switches that you think might make sense for the following careers in the Environmental Careers cluster:

1. Florist _____

2. Landscape architect _____

3. Farmer _____

4. Soil analyst _____

5. Conservationist _____

FRINGE BENEFITS Select a hobby that might turn into an environmental career and draw a three-stage picture showing the development of the career.

30

BEST BUYS

Select three items you would like to have in this store. For each "purchase" tell why you chose it, what you will do with it and name careers related to each.

chemistry set
telescope
guitar
bicycle
baby doll
movie camera
pool
encylopedia
typewriter
paint and an easel
skis
tape recorder
sled
sewing machine
rocket set
bat and ball
stamp book and stamps
television
skate board
basketball set
tool kit

Item I want	Why I want the item	What I will do with it	A related career

31

WRITERS' WORKSHOP

Use the space below to develop the outline of a script for a play, a musical comedy, a short film presentation or a television special that you would like to see publicly produced.

Title:

Cast:

Time:

Place:

Theme:

Beginning:

Climax:

Use the back of this paper to write the entire script.

FRINGE BENEFITS: Plan costumes, stage settings and publicity releases for your production.

DIRECTING DUTIES

You are the office manager and must assign this list of duties to the right office workers. Write the tasks on the spaces provided on each desk.

type letters	prepare taxes	write newspaper statements
make appointments	write pay checks	answer telephone
take dictation		work on advertising

Public Relations
Duties for the Day:
1. _____
2. _____

Accountant
Duties for the day:
1. _____
2. _____

Receptionist
Duties for the day:
1. _____
2. _____

Secretary
Duties for the day:
1. _____
2. _____

FRINGE BENEFITS Use your imagination. Assign another duty to each office worker.

OCEAN NOTIONS

Use crayons or pastel chalk to draw an underwater scene in the space below. Show one of the following marine science career situations in your picture.

- Deep Sea Diver
- Ocean Fishing Boat Operator
- Underwater Construction Worker
- Underwater Salvage Operator
- Marine Animal Researcher
- Underwater Demolition Worker

FRINGE BENEFITS Use an encyclopedia or other resource books for information to write the role description of a deep sea diver, a fish hatcher and raiser or an oceanographic mapper.

34

SPECIAL DELIVERY

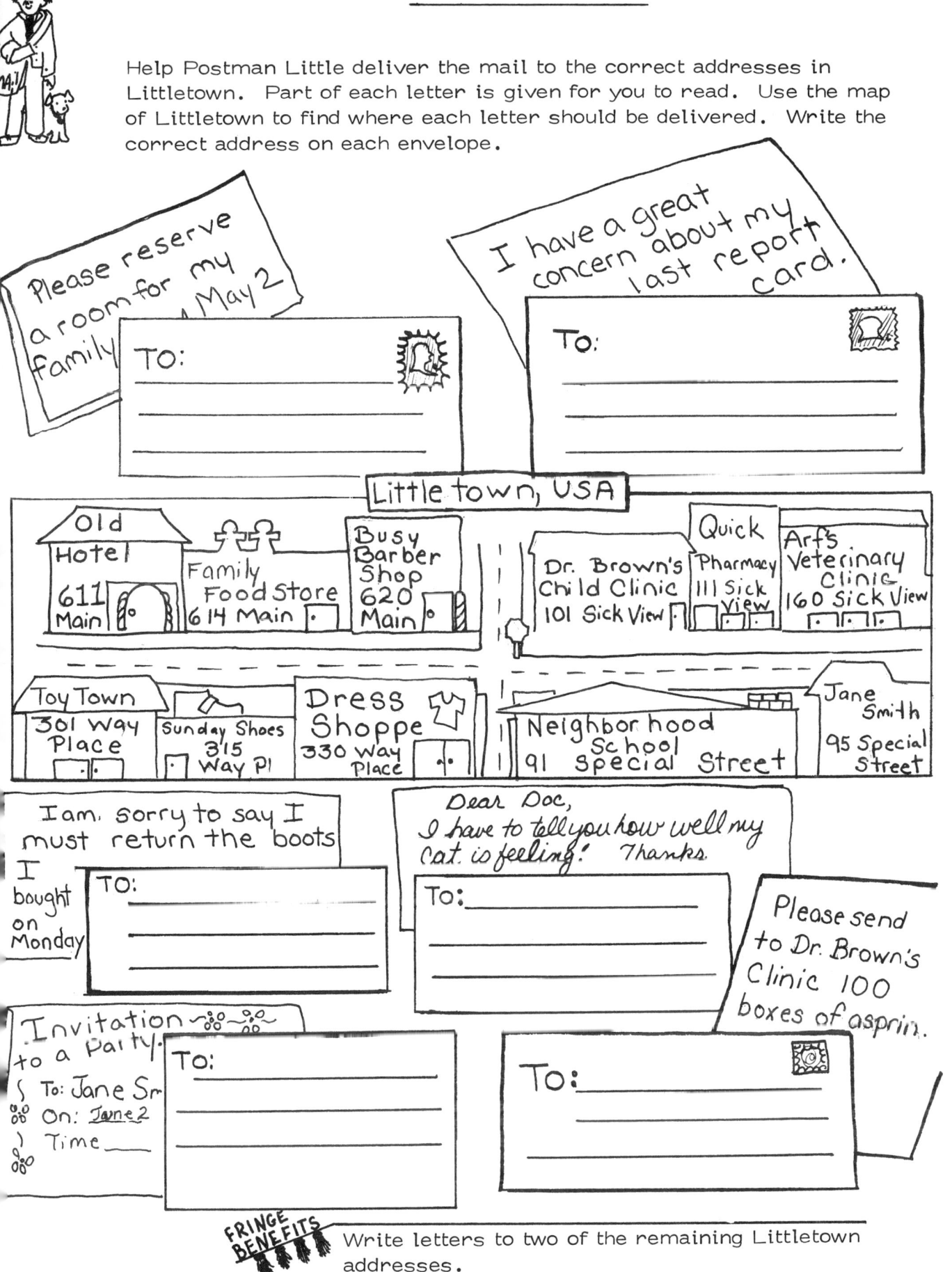

Help Postman Little deliver the mail to the correct addresses in Littletown. Part of each letter is given for you to read. Use the map of Littletown to find where each letter should be delivered. Write the correct address on each envelope.

Please reserve a room for my family May 2

TO: _____

I have a great concern about my last report card.

TO: _____

Littletown, USA

- Old Hotel 611 Main
- Family Food Store 614 Main
- Busy Barber Shop 620 Main
- Dr. Brown's Child Clinic 101 Sick View
- Quick Pharmacy 111 Sick View
- Arf's Veterinary Clinic 160 Sick View
- Toy Town 301 Way Place
- Sunday Shoes 315 Way Pl
- Dress Shoppe 330 Way Place
- Neighborhood School 91 Special Street
- Jane Smith 95 Special Street

I am sorry to say I must return the boots I bought on Monday

TO: _____

Dear Doc, I have to tell you how well my cat is feeling! Thanks.

TO: _____

Please send to Dr. Brown's Clinic 100 boxes of aspirin.

*Invitation to a Party
To: Jane Sm
On: June 2
Time ____*

TO: _____

TO: _____

FRINGE BENEFITS — Write letters to two of the remaining Littletown addresses.

35

CONSUMER GUIDE

Use your dictionary to find the definition of a consumer. As a consumer, tell where you might secure the goods or services on this list..

Week of _____

Things to do	Where	Workers Involved
1 Cash a check		
2 Get a hair cut		
3 Buy party invitations		
4 Have teeth cleaned		
5 Buy groceries		
6 Have radio repaired		
7 Have bracelet engraved		
8 Have clothes cleaned		
9 Order birthday cake		

Make your own weekly list of things you need to do as a consumer. Name the workers you will come in contact with during your shopping spree.

MAKING TRACKS

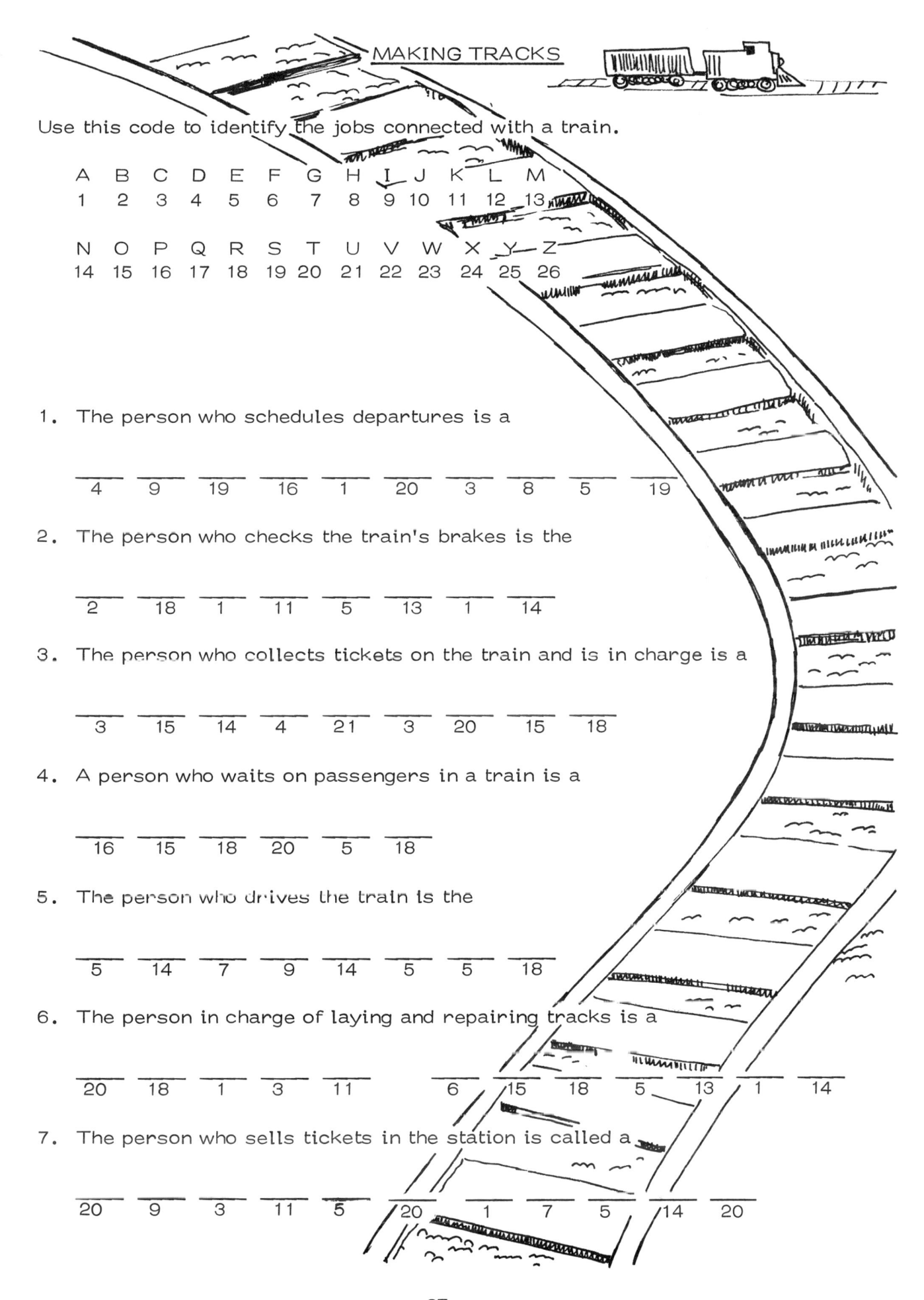

Use this code to identify the jobs connected with a train.

A	B	C	D	E	F	G	H	I	J	K	L	M
1	2	3	4	5	6	7	8	9	10	11	12	13

N	O	P	Q	R	S	T	U	V	W	X	Y	Z
14	15	16	17	18	19	20	21	22	23	24	25	26

1. The person who schedules departures is a

   __ __ __ __ __ __ __ __ __ __
   4 9 19 16 1 20 3 8 5 19

2. The person who checks the train's brakes is the

   __ __ __ __ __ __ __ __
   2 18 1 11 5 13 1 14

3. The person who collects tickets on the train and is in charge is a

   __ __ __ __ __ __ __ __ __
   3 15 14 4 21 3 20 15 18

4. A person who waits on passengers in a train is a

   __ __ __ __ __ __
   16 15 18 20 5 18

5. The person who drives the train is the

   __ __ __ __ __ __ __ __
   5 14 7 9 14 5 5 18

6. The person in charge of laying and repairing tracks is a

   __ __ __ __ __ __ __ __ __ __ __ __
   20 18 1 3 11   6 15 18 5 13 1 14

7. The person who sells tickets in the station is called a

   __ __ __ __ __ __ __ __ __ __ __
   20 9 3 11 5 20 1 7 5 14 20

NATURAL RESOURCE SCRAMBLE

Unscramble these words to identify Agriculture and Natural Resource occupations. (Note: Look for the letter and hidden picture hints.)

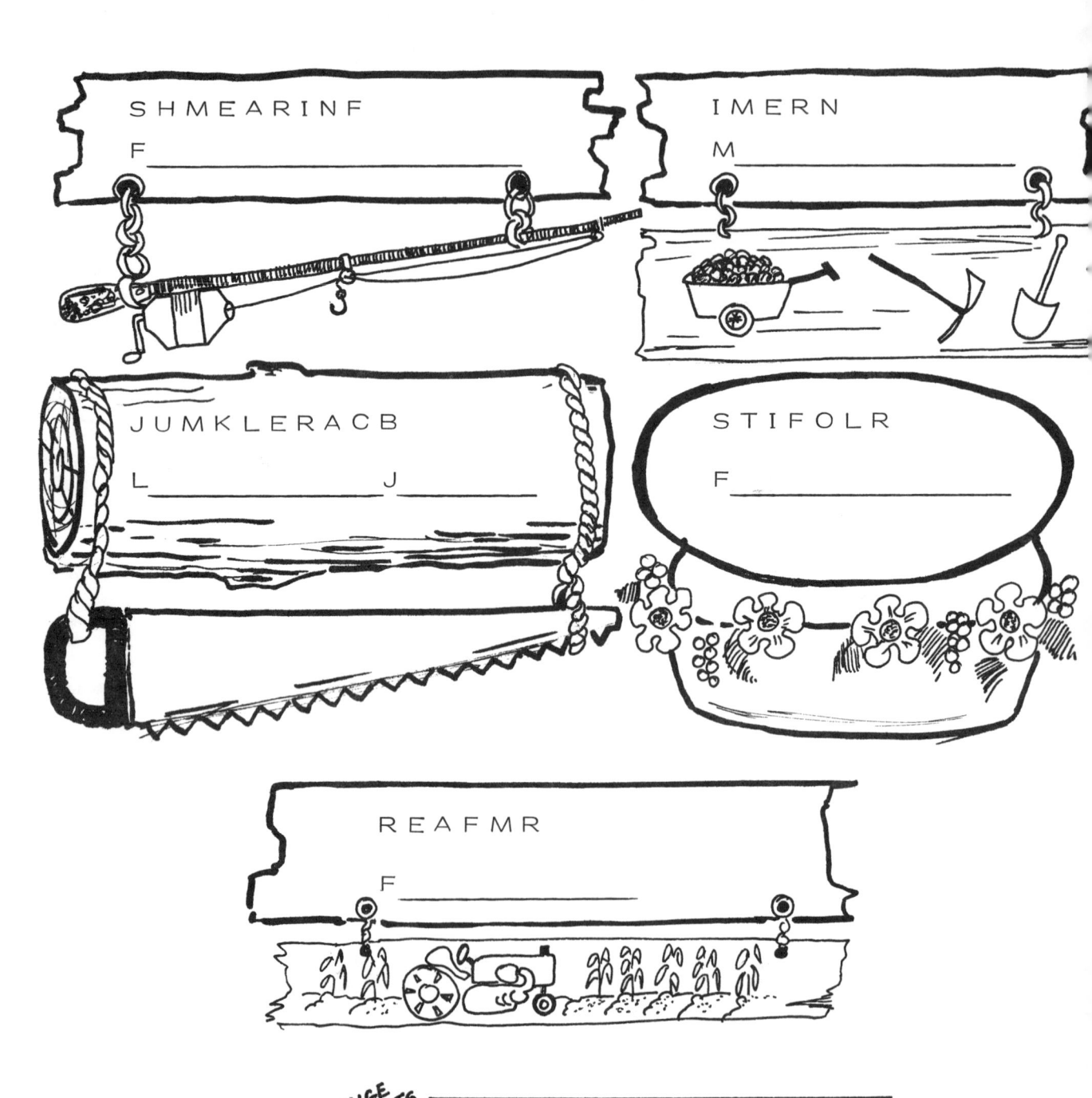

SHMEARINF

F _____

IMERN

M _____

JUMKLERACB

L _____ J _____

STIFOLR

F _____

REAFMR

F _____

FRINGE BENEFITS — Design signs for these occupations:

- Geologist
- Harvester
- Logger
- Ranger
- Oil Driller
- Forester
- Botanist
- Soil Conservationist
- Landscape Architect
- Trapper

TURNABOUT TEACHER

Find out about a teacher's job. Imagine that today is a "turnabout day" and you are the teacher in your classroom. Plan the day's lessons and activities by completing this "Turnabout Teacher" planning sheet.

Teacher Planning Book

Date _____

Goals for the day:
_____
_____
_____

Daily Schedule

Time	Activities	Materials needed
9:00		
10:00		
11:00		
12:00		
1:00		
2:00		
3:00		

🍎 **Notes and Special things:**

FRINGE BENEFITS — Find out how another worker in the school plans his days. Interview him and complete a written daily schedule.

39

A CAREER IS BORN

Discover more about a career of your choice by writing a historical account of how your career began. Use reference materials to assist you in the search. Include the following information: when the career began, the people or events that influenced its beginning, the tools used, interesting aspects of the career, what the working day was like, uniforms or clothing worn, special skills needed and training or education needed.

The History of _____
(career)

Make a collage to show your ideas about the future of this career.

BUILDING CAREERS

If a carpenter makes door frames, color the #1 spaces.
If a carpenter hangs wallpaper, color the #2 spaces.
If a carpenter installs plumbing, color the #3 spaces.
If a carpenter builds stairs, color the #4 spaces.
If a carpenter puts up walls, color the #5 spaces.
If a roofer lays blocks, color the #6 spaces.
If a roofer uses shingles, color the #7 spaces.
If a roofer mixes concrete, color the #8 spaces.
If an electrician installs insulation, color the #9 spaces.
If an electrician installs siding, color the #10 spaces.
If an electrician installs wiring and circuit breakers, color the #11 spaces.
If a mason builds foundations, color the #12 spaces.
If a mason mixes concrete and mortar, color the #13 spaces.
If a mason installs furnaces, color the #14 spaces.
If an architect designs buildings, color the #15 spaces.

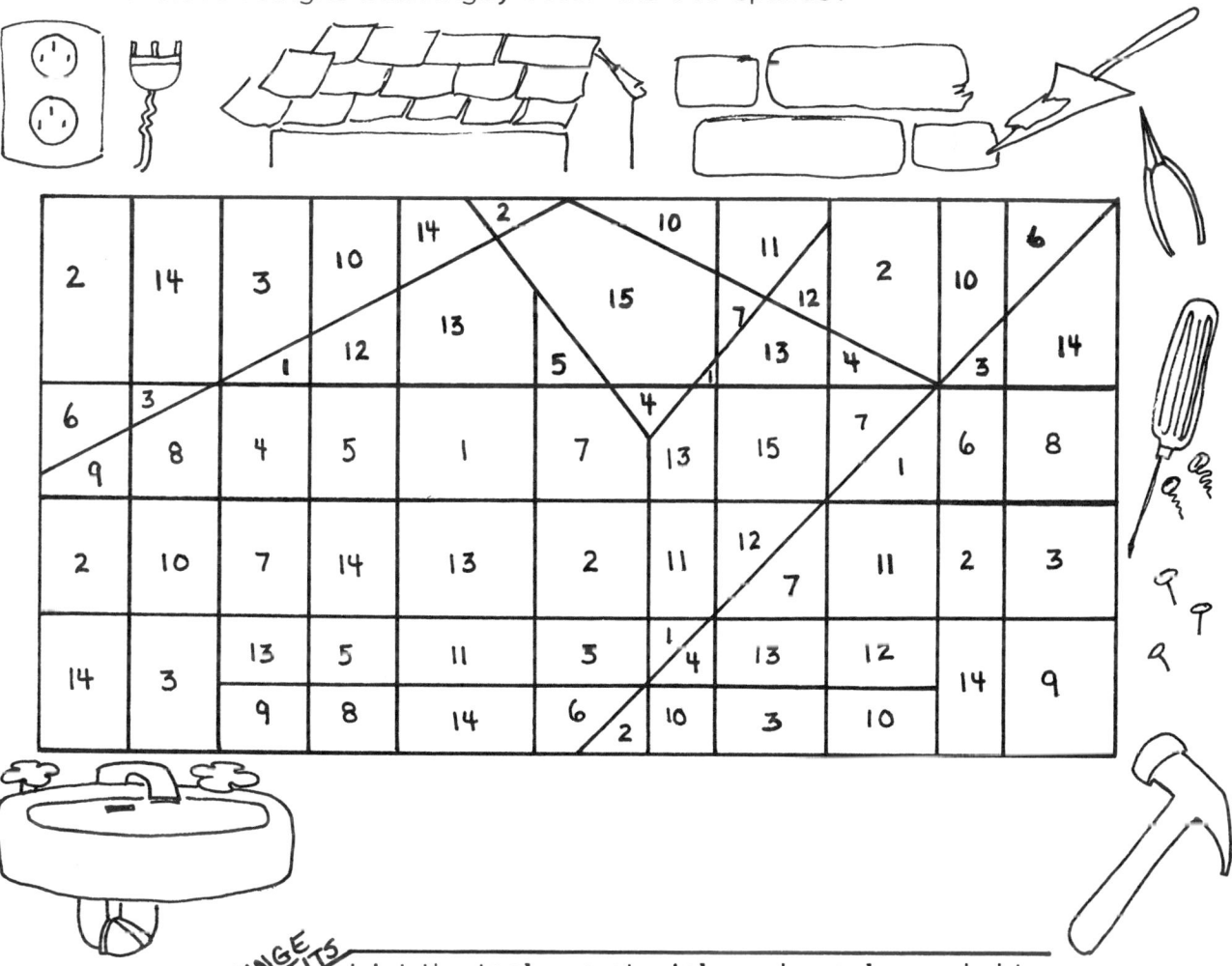

FRINGE BENEFITS List the tools, materials and people needed to construct a building.

41

COMMON CLUSTERS

Beside each "cluster" of occupations write what the people who hold the occupations must have in common.

Florists, Farmers, Foresters

Must enjoy:
_____

Must be good at:
_____

Carpenters, Roofers, House Painters

Must enjoy:
_____

Must be good at:
_____

Zoo Keepers, Veterinarians, Kennel Workers

Must enjoy:
_____

Must be good at:
_____

Cashiers, Bank Tellers, Ticket Agents

Must enjoy:
_____

Must be good at:
_____

Teachers, Camp Counselors, Day Care Workers

Must enjoy:
_____

Must be good at:
_____

OH YES GIRLS CAN!

Women now hold many jobs that were once thought to be occupations held chiefly by men. Examples of such occupations are:

physician	engineer	construction worker
lawyer	mechanic	police officer
mail carrier	banker	pharmacist

1. Choose three of the occupations listed above and write their names in the "office" door space.

2. List four skills needed for each occupation chosen.

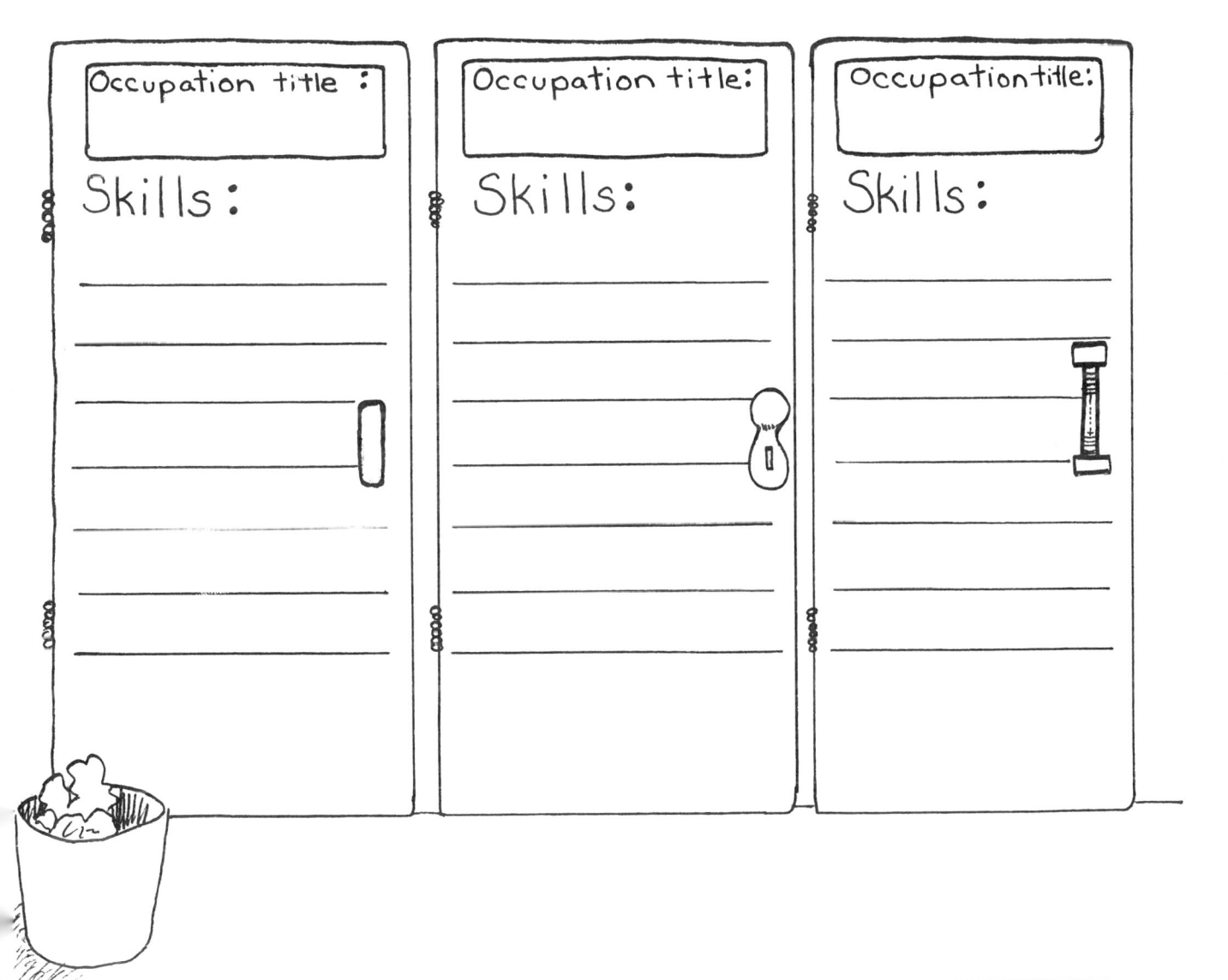

Occupation title: Occupation title: Occupation title:

Skills: Skills: Skills:

Work with a friend. Think of two other occupations which women may have as a career. Illustrate the occupations.

43

INTER-OFFICE MEMO

Pretend you are the office manager for a very large publishing company. It is your responsibility to recruit, hire and train the entire office staff. Write role descriptions to send to the employment agency for the following vacancies in your office.

Memo
Stenographer

Memo
Accountant

Memo
Systems Analyst

Memo
General Office Clerk

FRINGE BENEFITS — Write an inter-office memo to send to encourage office employees to correct tardiness, stop office gossip and shorten long coffee breaks.

BEAUTY-FULL JOBS

Write the job title of each person responsible for the "make-over" of Millie the Model. (The arrows provide clues.) List three tools the workers might use in each process.

Jobs to use: Seamstress   Manicurist   Cosmetologist
               Hair Stylist   Fashion Consultant

Before   ## After

Job: _____
Tools:
 1. _____
 2. _____
 3. _____

Job: _____
Tools:
 1. _____
 2. _____
 3. _____

Job: _____
Tools:
 1. _____
 2. _____
 3. _____

Job: _____
Tools:
 1. _____
 2. _____
 3. _____

Job: _____
Tools:
 1. _____
 2. _____
 3. _____

FRINGE BENEFITS — Draw "before" and "after" pictures of Stu the Star. List the workers involved in the "makeover."

COMMUNICATION EXPLORATION

Explore the career possibilities in the world of communication. List and describe the job opportunities in the following areas:

Television Careers
Job Title   Job Description

1. _____   _____
2. _____   _____
3. _____   _____

Radio Careers
Job Title

1. _____   _____
2. _____   _____
3. _____   _____

Newspaper Careers
Job Title

1. _____   _____
2. _____   _____
3. _____   _____

Writing Careers (Books and Magazines)
Job Title

1. _____   _____
2. _____   _____
3. _____   _____

Film Making and Photography Careers
Job Title

1. _____   _____
2. _____   _____
3. _____   _____

FRINGE BENEFITS Learn more about a communication career you think you might enjoy. Describe the skills, training and job opportunities associated with your chosen career.

PAPER CONNECTIONS

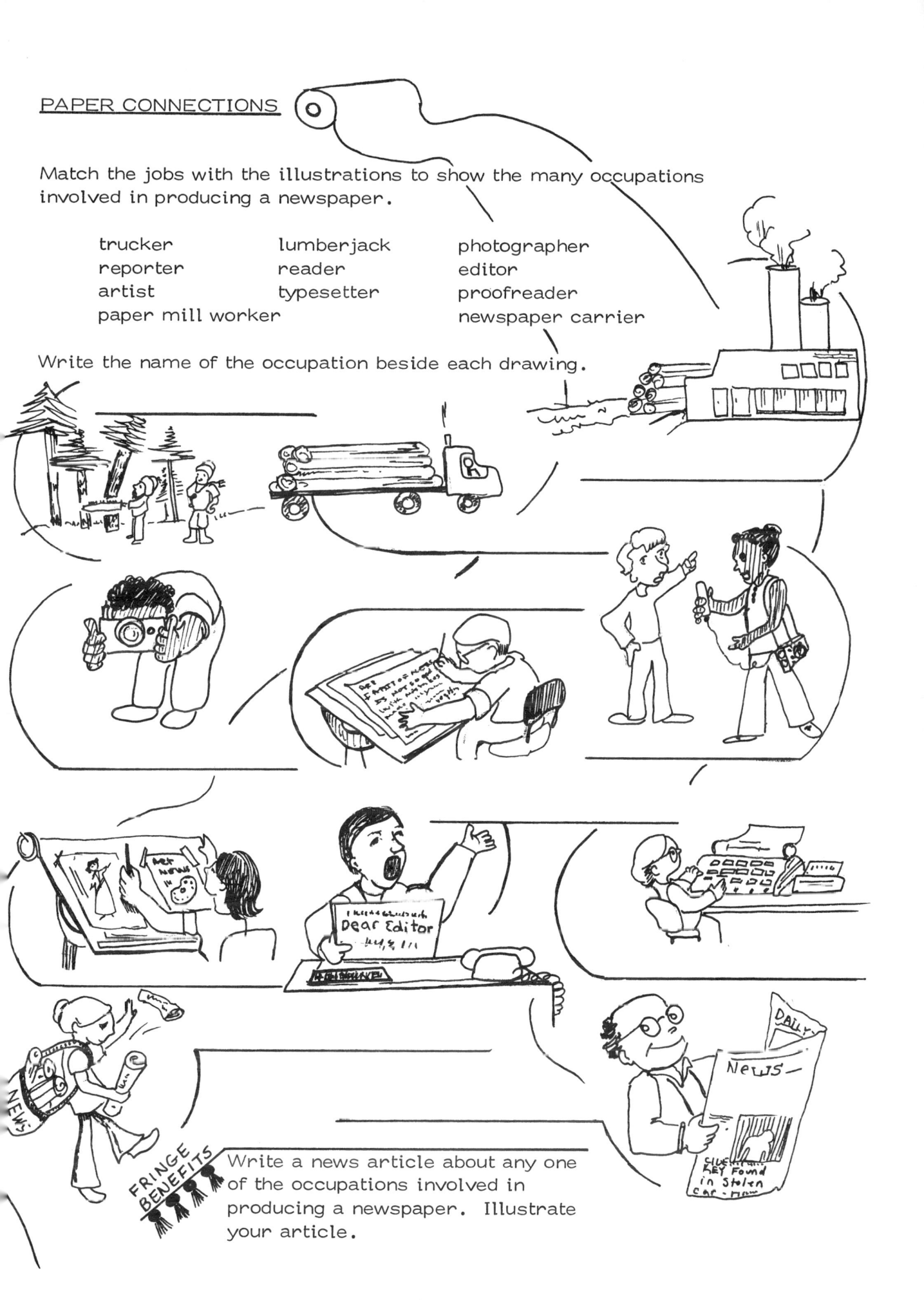

Match the jobs with the illustrations to show the many occupations involved in producing a newspaper.

trucker	lumberjack	photographer
reporter	reader	editor
artist	typesetter	proofreader
paper mill worker		newspaper carrier

Write the name of the occupation beside each drawing.

Write a news article about any one of the occupations involved in producing a newspaper. Illustrate your article.

FRINGE BENEFITS

WHO KNOWS IT?

barber, roofer, chef, tailor, tutor, clerk, engineer, judge, accountant, nurse

Match the careers with their knowledge requirements. Write each career name in its correct crossword space.

Across

1. Knowledge of fabrics and patterns
3. Knowledge of food and recipes
5. Knowledge of school subjects
7. Knowledge of design and building
9. Knowledge of the law

Down

2. Knowledge of merchandise
4. Knowledge of hairstyles
6. Knowledge of mathematics
8. Knowledge of shingles and roofs
10. Knowledge of medicine

FRINGE BENEFITS

Make your own crossword puzzles using the following occupations:

Puzzle 1
florist
farmer
teacher
model

Puzzle 2
carpenter
actor
dentist
cashier

Write a knowledge list for your puzzles and have a friend supply the answers.

48

DEVICE DEPENDENCE

We depend upon many machines and devices to assist us in our daily lives. Imagine that each of the following situations are true. Tell what effect these will have, and list optional ways of providing the same services.

Situation:

There are no refrigerators.

Effect: _____
_____
_____
_____
_____

Service Alternatives:
1. _____
2. _____
3. _____

Situation:

There are no automobiles.

Effect: _____
_____
_____
_____
_____

Service Alternatives:
1. _____
2. _____
3. _____

Situation:

There are no televisions.

Effect: _____
_____
_____
_____
_____

Service Alternatives:
1. _____
2. _____
3. _____

Situation:

There are no telephones.

Effect: _____
_____
_____
_____
_____

Service Alternatives:
1. _____
2. _____
3. _____

Situation:

There is no electricity.

Effect: _____
_____
_____
_____
_____

Service Alternatives:
1. _____
2. _____
3. _____

Situation:

There are no washing machines.

Effect: _____
_____
_____
_____
_____

Service Alternatives:
1. _____
2. _____
3. _____

FRINGE BENEFITS Illustrate a situation in which a broken machine affected your life.

49

MOVE-MEANT

Unscramble these careers in transportation and describe the job duties for each.

r u k c t e r - _ _ _ _ _ _ _

Job duties: _____
_____
_____
_____

i p o l t - _ _ _ _ _ _

Job duties: _____
_____
_____
_____

a x t i a b c r i d v e r - _ _ _ _ _ _ _ _ _ _ _ _ _ _

Job duties: _____
_____
_____

u b s r i d v r e - _ _ _ _ _ _ _ _ _

Job duties: _____
_____
_____
_____

b o t a p t c a i a n - _ _ _ _ _ _ _ _ _ _ _

Job duties: _____
_____
_____

f a f h e c u r u - _ _ _ _ _ _ _ _

Job duties: _____
_____
_____
_____

FRINGE BENEFITS Identify three possible transportation careers of the future and describe the job duties for each.

50

SCRAMBLED SUMMERS

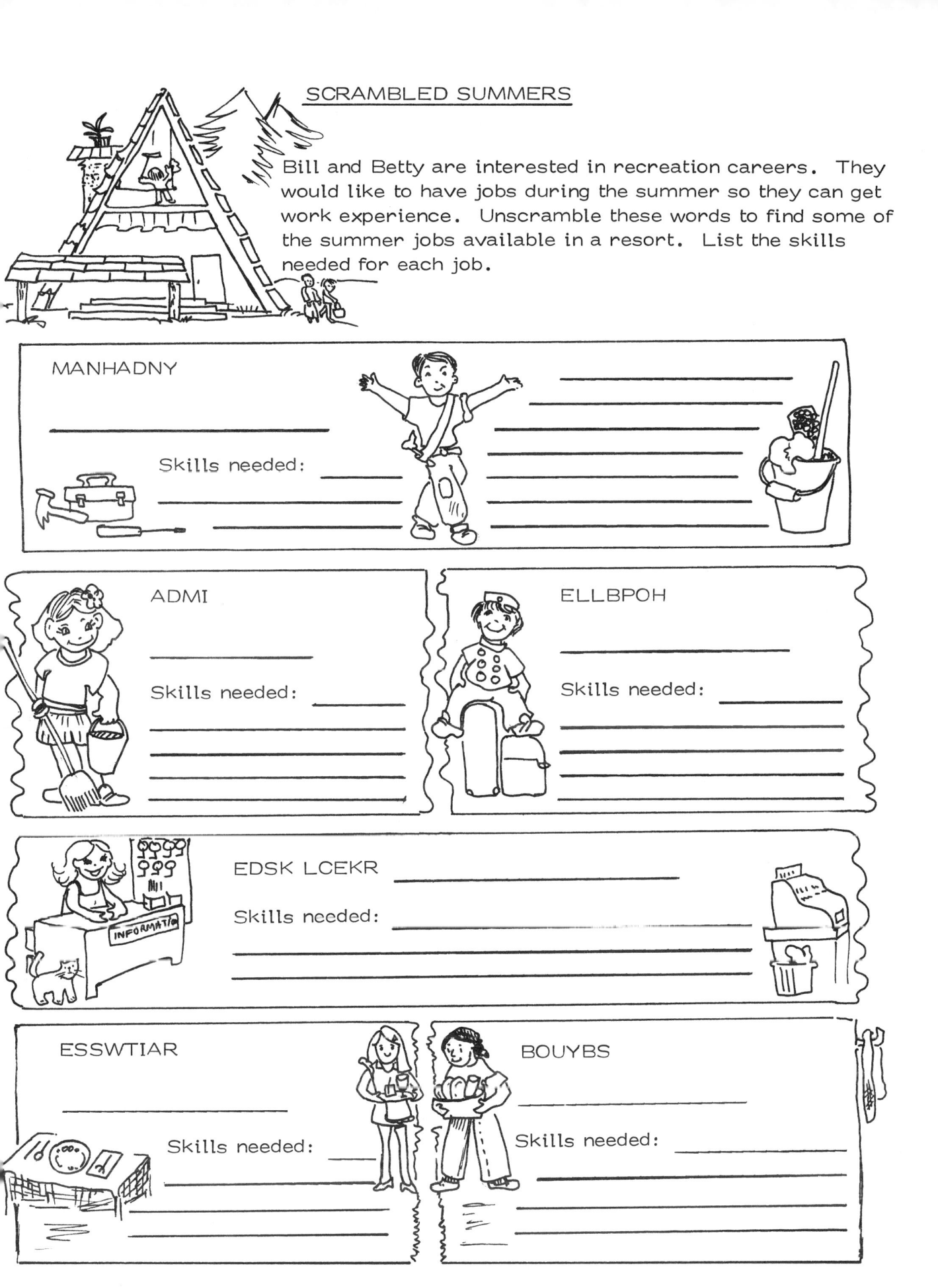

Bill and Betty are interested in recreation careers. They would like to have jobs during the summer so they can get work experience. Unscramble these words to find some of the summer jobs available in a resort. List the skills needed for each job.

MANHADNY _____

Skills needed: _____
_____
_____

ADMI _____

Skills needed: _____
_____
_____
_____

ELLBPOH _____

Skills needed: _____
_____
_____
_____

EDSK LCEKR _____

Skills needed: _____
_____
_____

ESSWTIAR _____

Skills needed: _____
_____
_____

BOUYBS _____

Skills needed: _____
_____
_____

51

TRY IT

Try being an advertiser. Choose a career and sell yourself and your skills by completing this billboard.

_____ **is my** name,
(Your name)
And _____ is my game.
        career
I am able to _____ _____ and
              (Skill) (Skill)
_____ with skill.
(Skill)
So go with me...
I'll fill the job bill!

you and your career
as   pictured.

Write a television or radio commercial "selling" your career (for example, "Be A Secretary," "Be A Teacher," "Be a Salesperson"). List three skills you will need for this career.

_____
_____
_____
_____

RIDDLING CAREERS

Read the riddles and write the occupation which answers each riddle in the space provided.

My razor and scissors I use with care,
You come to me to cut your hair.
Who am I? _____

I use colors of reds, greens and blues,
And make your house the color you choose.
Who am I? _____

I make cookies, cakes and breads.
You come to me when you want to be fed.
Who am I? _____

By holding up my hand I can show
When the traffic should stop and go.
Who am I? _____

I fill the tank with gasoline in the job I do.
I put air in the tires, and check the battery, too.
Who am I? _____

I sing and dance until my job is done.
The purpose of my career is for you to have fun.
Who am I? _____

I work with wires and current to brighten your night.
My skills allow you to flip the switch and turn on the light.
Who am I? _____

I use paper, books and chalk to show
What every boy and girl should know.
Who am I? _____

I teach how to throw the ball
And when you tumble, how not to fall.
Who am I? _____

FRINGE BENEFITS Work with a friend. Make up three occupation riddles. Give them to classmates to answer.

HELP WANTED

Use the Help Wanted ads to help the people in the Work Wanted ads find the best jobs available. Give reasons for your choice.

HELP WANTED ADS

Bookkeeper: Full or part-time. Exp. in accounts payable & receivable. Need good typing skills. Apply: In The Red Co., 531 Park.	**Machinist:** Experienced, able to travel, good pay & benefits. Apply: Gear Getters, Inc. 1490 Lathe Lane.	**Manager Trainee:** Growing company is seeking person with college degree. Will train. Experience helpful but not a must. Call for Mrs. Trained at 555-4781.	**Manager's Ass't:** For ladies' dress store. Must be experienced in sales & management. Excellent opportunity for agressive person. Call M. Dresser at 555-4950.
Service Station Att.: Must be dependable & honest. No phone calls. Apply at station. Green Gas Station, #5 Motor Blvd. after 12 noon only.	**Receptionist:** Typing skills, pleasant personality, ability to meet & deal with people. Send resume & reference letters to Mr. Smiles, #4 Pleasant Place.	**Machinist:** Must be able to set up & operate lathes, mills, etc. Day shift. Call between 9-11 a.m. at 1-555-8134.	**Service Station Att.:** Dependable worker with tow truck experience. Send application to Mr. D. Fuel at 47891 Gasoline Alley.

WORK WANTED ADS	Best Job To Apply For:	Reasons For Your Choice:
Wanted – position as bookkeeper/receptionist; full or part-time, good typing skills, enjoys working with public.		
Work Wanted – machine operator, high school graduate with experience desires day work, no travel.		
Wants job – as store manager, college degree, aggressive, no sales experience.		
Wanted: High school student desires summer job in service station, no experience, but dependable and willing to learn.		

FOR BOYS TOO!

Men now do many jobs that were once thought to be occupations held chiefly by women. Examples of such occupations are:

nurse	file clerk	child care worker
model	dressmaker	telephone operator
beautician	secretary	flight attendant

1. Choose three of the occupations listed and write their names on the lunch box "name plates" below.

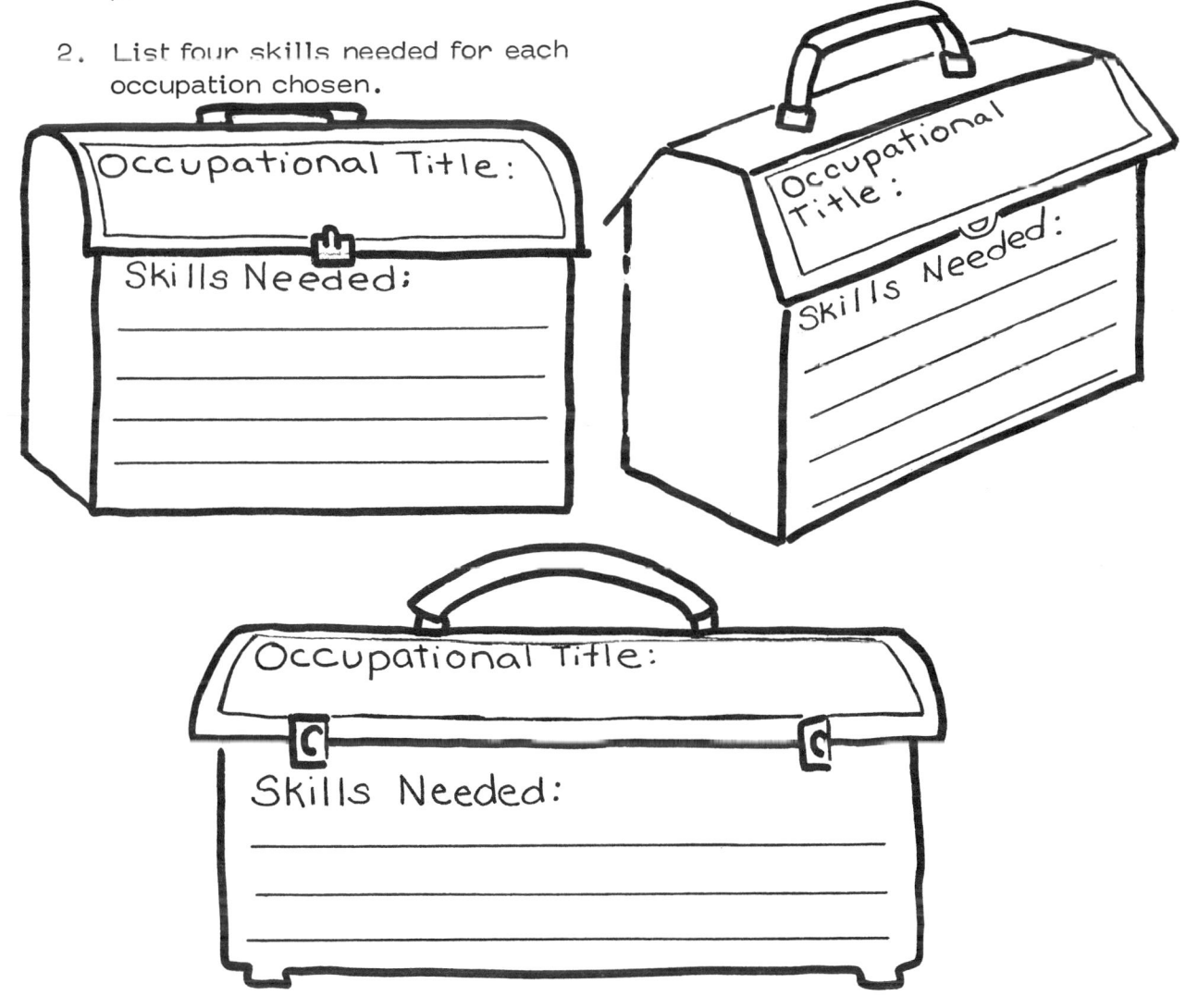

2. List four skills needed for each occupation chosen.

Occupational Title:
Skills Needed:
_____
_____
_____
_____

Occupational Title:
Skills Needed:
_____
_____
_____
_____

Occupational Title:
Skills Needed:
_____
_____
_____
_____

FRINGE BENEFITS — For each of the occupations chosen, list three "tools of the trade."

HOSPITAL HUNT

Find and circle the "jobs in a hospital" hidden in the puzzle.

```
e g m p n j e d s t r a t
m l e h (h o s p i t a l) g
l a d y s b t c f o z a x
n u r s e s a i d e l d r
a u d i o l o g i s t m a
d m o c s a e r g d e i y
s e c a i b s b k i c n t
t d s l c w r a b e h i e
c l o t k o u f s t n s c
a c p h a r m a c i s t h
g i r e j k n x t c c r n
p n o r d e r l y i b a i
i e h a i r q u m a s t c
r x e p w o m v b n a o i
f l b i m z a s k i l r a
p h y s i c i a n f t o n
t w e t n g d e n t i s t
```

Words to find:

administrator   maid   physician
audiologist   nurse's aide   x-ray technician
dentist   orderly   dietician
pharmacist   lab worker   physical therapist

List other jobs you might find in a hospital.

_____

_____

_____

FRINGE BENEFITS

Describe what duties these hospital workers perform. Use resource materials if needed.

CHORE CHECK

List below the jobs that have to be done in your home, in the rooms and in the yard. Next to each job, write the name of the "homeworker" who is responsible for getting the job done. Complete the job tally by writing the names of members of your family and the number of home jobs they do.

Bathroom Jobs	Homeworker	Bedroom Jobs	Homeworker

Kitchen Jobs	Homeworker	Living Room Jobs	Homeworker

Outdoor Jobs	Home-Worker

FAMILY JOB TALLY

Name	Number of jobs	How can I help?

FRINGE BENEFITS List five ways you depend upon your family for daily living needs.

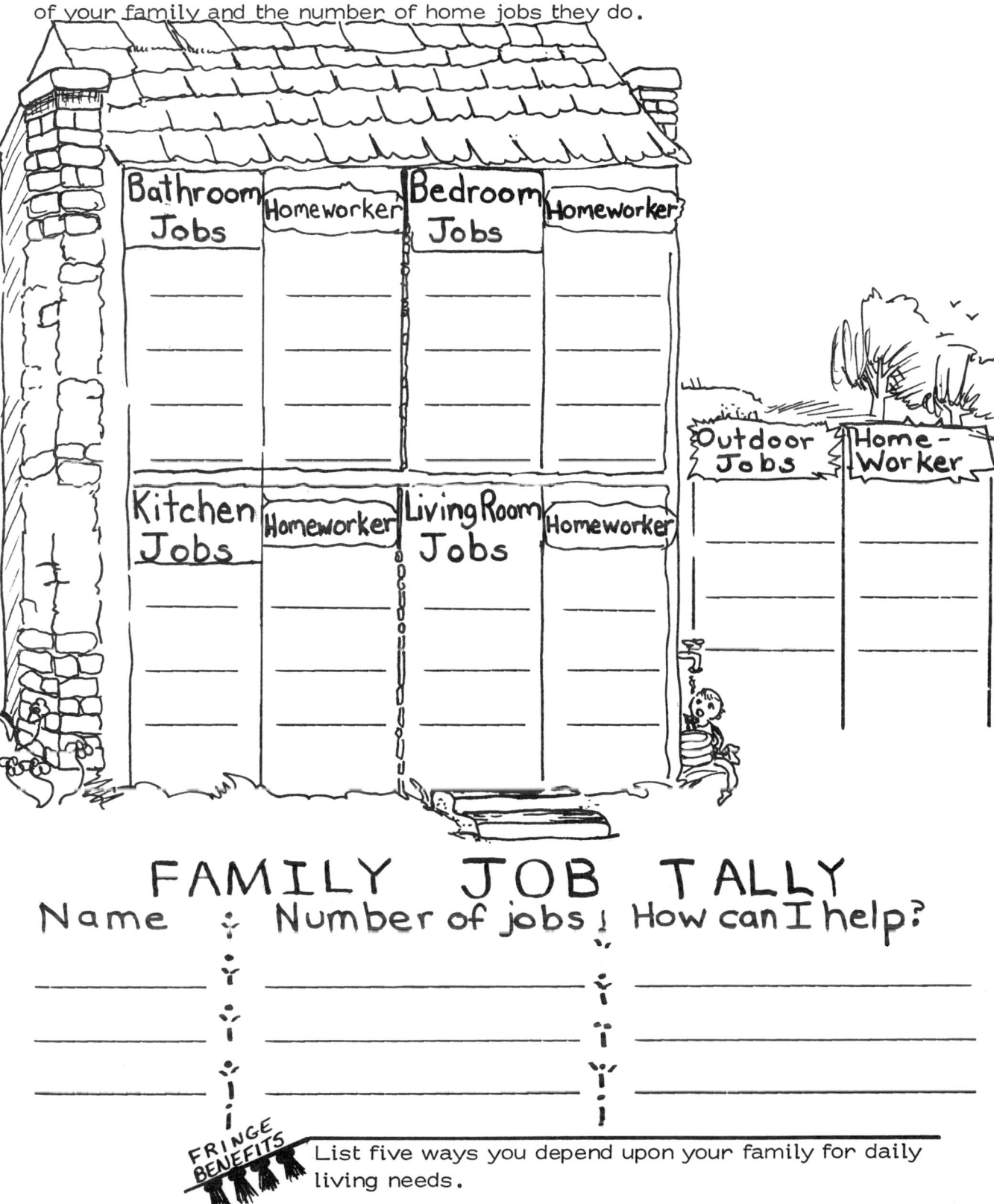

SPORT PROS

List two jobs connected with the sport pictured in each box below and name a special skill needed to be a "pro."

Some possible sports-related job choices are:

coach	referee	sports announcer	cashier
player	umpire	caddy	assistants
	clean-up crew member	bat boy	

Box 1 (football):
Job #1 _____
Skill _____
Job #2 _____
Skill _____

Box 2 (tennis):
Job #1 _____
Skill _____
Job #2 _____
Skill _____

Box 3 (swimming/diving):
Job #1 _____
Skill _____
Job #2 _____
Skill _____

Box 4 (baseball):
Job #1 _____
Skill _____
Job #2 _____
Skill _____

Box 5 (golf):
Job #1 _____
Skill _____
Job #2 _____
Skill _____

Box 6 (bowling):
Job #1 _____
Skill _____
Job #2 _____
Skill _____

FRINGE BENEFITS — Draw your own sports illustrations and name the jobs!

JOB COUNSELOR

Be a job counselor and help these people choose a job. Read the description of each job seeker. Choose a job to match the person's skills and interests. Write a sentence to explain the reasons for your choice. (Use your **imagination**!! Remember, there is no one correct answer.)

Sue likes fashions and enjoys wearing clothes. Her hobby is designing and sewing her own creations. She is artistic and likes to work with colorful fabrics. She might like to be a _____ because _____
_____
_____.

Steve likes food. He <u>really</u> likes food! He likes to make up his own recipes. He enjoys cooking and serving his "taste" treats to friends. Steve might like to be a _____ because _____
_____
_____
_____

Tom likes the outdoor life. He enjoys camping, hiking and nature. His favorite subjects in school were botany, biology and zoology. He was a Boy Scout and a summer camper. He likes working with children and teaching them how to enjoy the outdoors. Tom might like to be a _____ because _____
_____
_____
_____
_____

Write a description of your own hobbies and skills. Give it to a friend and have him or her choose a possible job for you.

SHOPS GALORE

What kinds of things do you like to buy? List four items you would buy in each of the stores illustrated on this page. Remember, the items are your own choice and may be different from those listed by classmates.

Coopers and Sons Food Market

Drug Store

Clothing for boys and girls

Toy Store

Hardtack Hardware

Melvins Records and Tapes

Fringe Benefits: List five other things you would like to buy. (They may be found in stores other than the ones shown above.) Use magazines, advertisements and the newspaper for ideas. Find out how much the items would cost.

MANUFACTURING MATCH

Factory workers produce goods we use every day such as paper towels, cars and clothes. Use this chart, which describes the five levels of factory workers, to answer the questions following the chart.

Factory Occupational Levels	Job Descriptions	Education or Suggested Training
Technician	Puts engineer's designs into action—may assist in development and designing of parts	High school plus two-year degree program at junior college or vocational school
Craftsperson	Makes the tools, molds, patterns and instruments needed in the production process	High school and apprenticeship (2-5 yrs.)
Skilled Worker	Makes, operates and assembles the machinery and equipment	Vocational or technical school; on the job training
Semi-skilled Worker	Runs the machines used in manufacturing; assembles parts	Brief on-the-job instruction
Unskilled Worker	Includes jobs requiring physical labor—digging, loading, mixing	No special training

1. Sue wants to assist in the designing of airplanes. What will her occupational level be? _____ What training will she need? _____

2. Brad likes sewing his own clothes. He wants to be a sewing machine operator. What will his occupational level be? _____ What training will he need? _____

3. John likes to build model cars from diagrams. He would like to become a foundry pattern maker and make patterns following a blueprint. What level worker will he be? _____ What training will he need? _____

4. Linda wants to assist in developing better computers. What level worker will see be? _____ What training will she need? _____

5. Claire, an auto assembly-line worker, has a job attaching fenders to cars. What level worker is she? _____

6. Buck is looking for a job loading and unloading trucks. What training will he need? _____

TRAVEL TALK

Tourism is big business all over the world today. In the space below, design a travel brochure to be mailed by your city's Chamber of Commerce to encourage tourists to visit your city. Be sure to include information about natural scenic attractions, hotel accommodations, theater productions and restaurants.

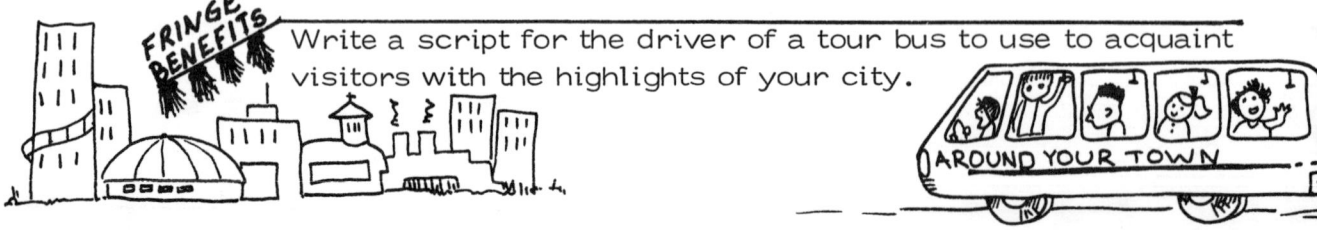

FRINGE BENEFITS — Write a script for the driver of a tour bus to use to acquaint visitors with the highlights of your city.

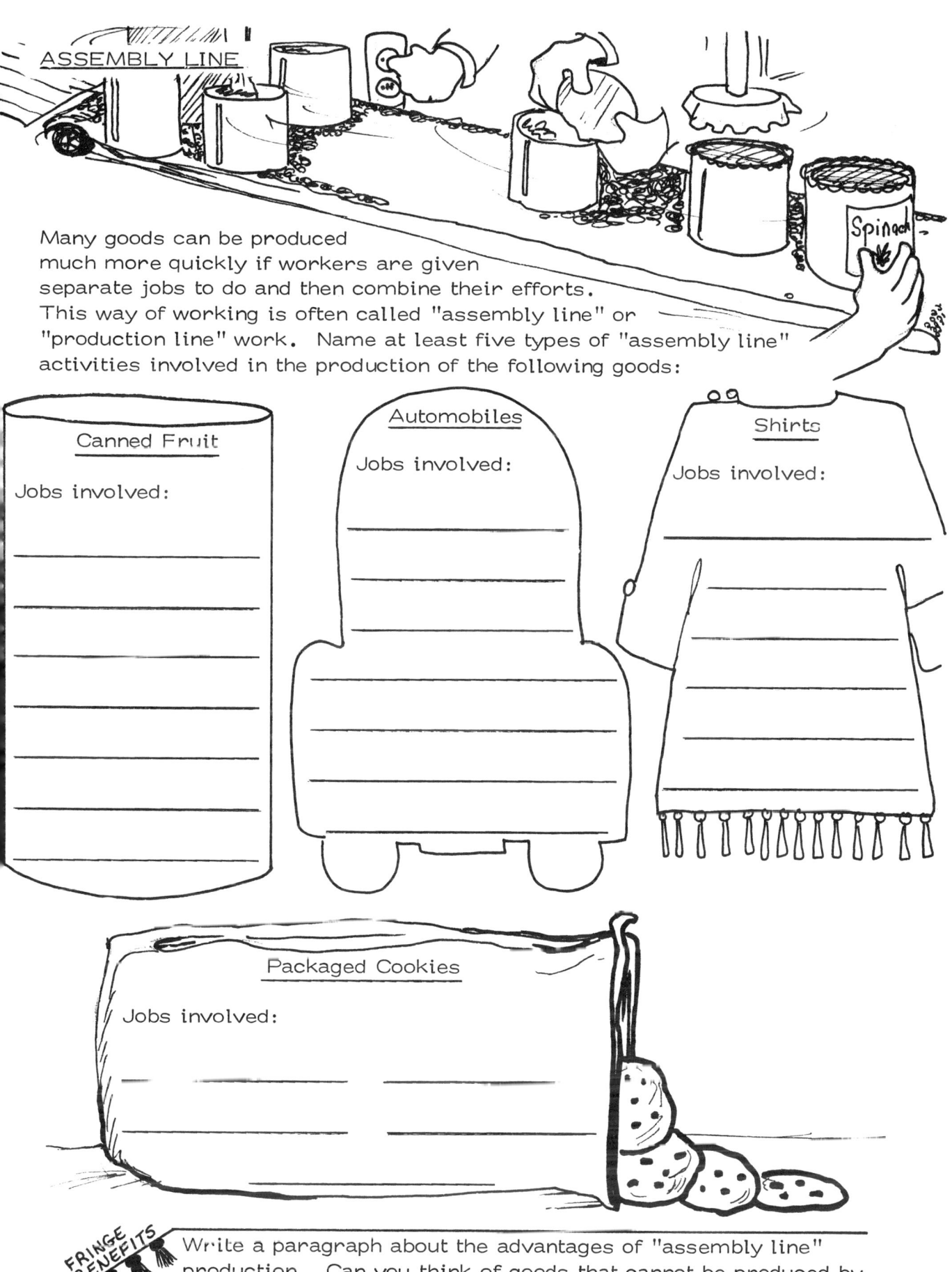

ASSEMBLY LINE

Many goods can be produced much more quickly if workers are given separate jobs to do and then combine their efforts. This way of working is often called "assembly line" or "production line" work. Name at least five types of "assembly line" activities involved in the production of the following goods:

Canned Fruit
Jobs involved:

_____
_____
_____
_____
_____
_____

Automobiles
Jobs involved:

_____
_____
_____
_____
_____
_____

Shirts
Jobs involved:

_____
_____
_____
_____
_____

Packaged Cookies
Jobs involved:

_____
_____
_____

FRINGE BENEFITS Write a paragraph about the advantages of "assembly line" production. Can you think of goods that cannot be produced by the "assembly line" method?

THE STORE

List the jobs available in a department store:

_____

_____

_____

_____

_____

_____

_____

_____

_____

THE STORE
Luncheonette

Beauty Salon | Personnel Hiring | The President
Ladies' Fashions MAKE UP Perfume | Credit Accounts | CASHIER
 | | Managerial Offices
Shoes | Teen Scene | FURS | KIDS KORNER | Men's Wear THE Young man
Purses | Babies' Wear | Alterations Tailoring |
Gift Wrap | TOYS AND MORE FUN | Fabric Center
Returns-Complaint Desk | CANDY | NOTIONS SEWING MACHINES

THE STORE

Jewelry | Hardware Home Supplies Garden Goods | Stationery, posters etc typewriters | Appliances CAMERAS Televisions and Stereos | Record Loft
Guard | | | |

Circle the job you like best and answer the following questions:

Why did you pick this job as your favorite? _____
_____

Do you think you would do well in this position? _____ Why? __
_____
_____
_____

examining human interdependence

NOTES

PROMISES, PROMISES

Read the imaginary situations below and write a sentence about the "probable" results of each forgotten promise.

You promised to feed Mrs. Jones' fish while she was on a trip. You forgot. What probably happened? _____
_____
_____

You promised to lock the gate after playing with the neighbor's dog. You forgot. What probably happened? _____
_____
_____

You promised to take care of the book you borrowed. You left it out in the yard and it rained! What probably happened? _____
_____

You promised to collect the mail for the Woods while they were on vacation. You forgot. What probably happened? _____
_____
_____

You promised to clean the living room before your mother got home from work. You watched television too long and didn't get around to the cleaning. Your mother came home with guests. What probably happened? _____
_____
_____

FRINGE BENEFITS You have big news to tell your best friend. Your friend promised to meet you after school, but went to the baseball game instead. Write a paragraph about how you feel.

67

PREDICTABLE CASUALTIES

Read each casualty card and write what probably happened in that situation. Write a second sentence describing the reactions of the people affected by the "undependable" action.

Casualty Card #1: Mr. Smith paid Roofer Brown to fix the hole in his roof. Roofer Brown did not complete his job duties. A big storm came from the west. What casualty probably occurred? _____

Casualty Card #2: Joe Driver ran through the red traffic light at the busy intersection. What casualty probably occurred? _____

Casualty Card #3: Sally Sue agreed to have her part for the big play memorized by Monday. She left her script at school and the school doors were locked for the weekend. What casualty probably occurred? _____

Casualty Card #4: Mrs. Smart depended on Mr. Smart to mail the electric bill. He forgot for three months in a row. What casualty probably occurred? _____

Casualty Card #5: Tim Camper neglected to make certain that his campfire was completely out before taking his hike. What casualty probably occurred? _____

Casualty Card #6: Ms. Lazy agreed to drive the school children to the train station so they could catch the 8:15 a.m. train to the zoo. It was the only train of the day. She did not wake up until 8:10. What casualty probably occurred? _____

MOVING CONNECTIONS

Identify the different people involved in each illustration. Write a sentence telling why each group must work together.

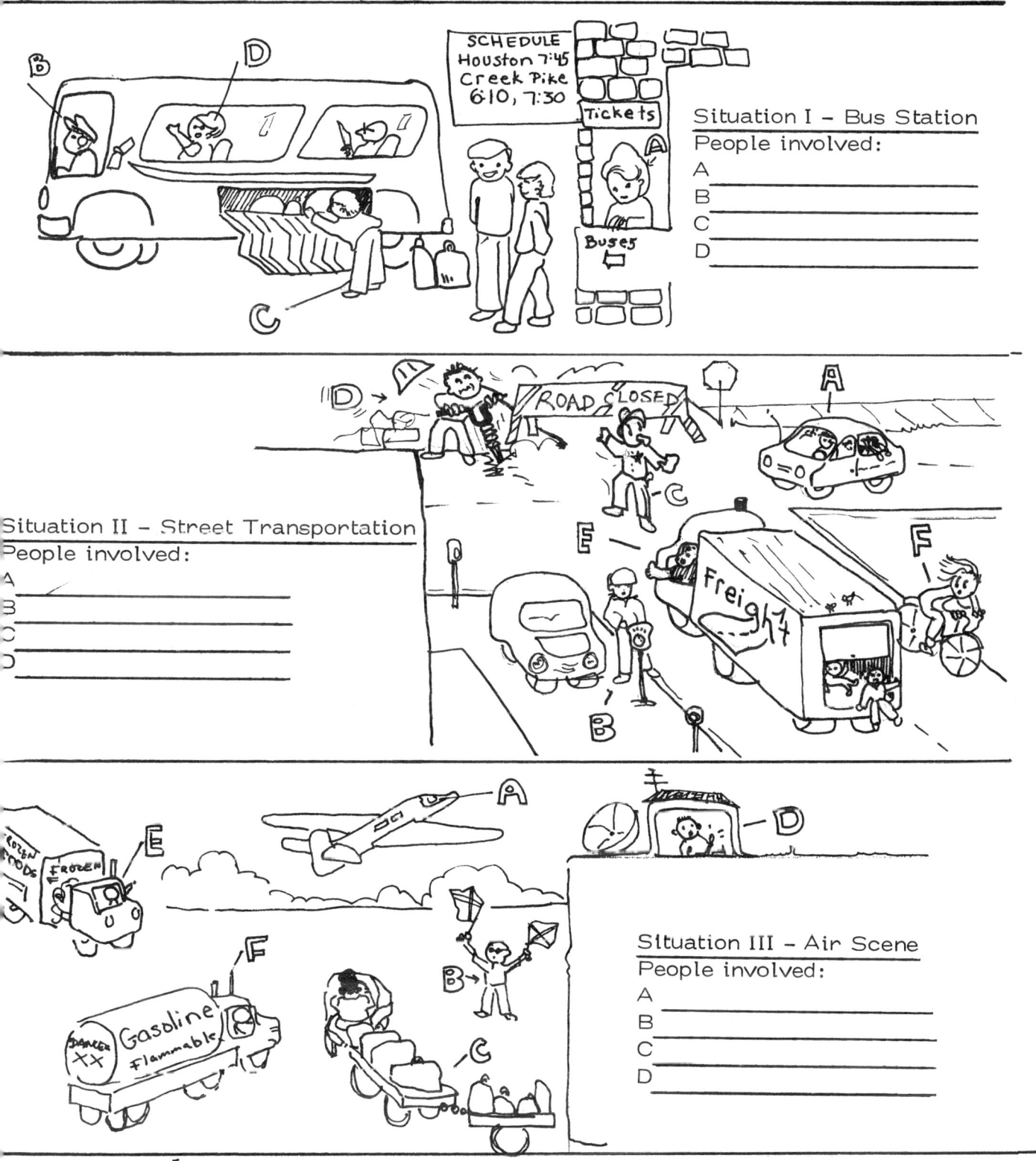

Situation I – Bus Station
People involved:
A _____
B _____
C _____
D _____

Situation II – Street Transportation
People involved:
A _____
B _____
C _____
D _____

Situation III – Air Scene
People involved:
A _____
B _____
C _____
D _____

FRINGE BENEFITS Use your experience. Describe in words or drawings another group of people who, even though each person might be doing a different task, must work together.

PARTY PLANNING

Your class is planning a party, and the duties involved need to be assigned. Complete this planning sheet by listing the things to be done by each group.

Groups

Refreshments

Decorations and Party Accessories

Guest List, Invitations and Publicity

Entertainment

Serving and Clean-Up

Responsibilities

Refreshments:
1. _____
2. _____
3. _____
4. _____
5. _____
6. _____

Decorations and Party Accessories:
1. _____
2. _____
3. _____
4. _____
5. _____
6. _____

Guest List, Invitations and Publicity:
1. _____
2. _____
3. _____
4. _____
5. _____
6. _____

Entertainment:
1. _____
2. _____
3. _____
4. _____
5. _____
6. _____

Serving and Clean-Up:
1. _____
2. _____
3. _____
4. _____
5. _____
6. _____

FRINGE BENEFITS Plan a special classroom party. Decide on a theme (Career Day, Future Day, etc.) and list the duties involved.

WORKING ATTITUDES

The way people feel about their jobs can affect how well they perform. Use this "Work Attitude Scale" to rate the workers' attitudes described below.

Work Attitude Scale

Ratings | Poor — Fair — Good!
          1   2   3

Worker No. 1

"I'm just doing this job for the summer, so why should I do my best? I'll just do what they tell me."

Attitude Rating _____

How will this attitude affect job performance?
_____
_____

Worker No. 2

"I'm glad I have this summer job because I'll need work experience to get the job I want. I'm going to prove to myself and others that I can be a good worker."

Attitude Rating _____

How will this attitude affect job performance?
_____
_____

Worker No. 3

"I don't like this job--it's just like the other ones I had this summer. Guess I'll quit! I can always find a better job."

Attitude Rating _____

How will this attitude affect job performance?
_____
_____

FRINGE BENEFITS Imagine you are an employer. Select the worker you would want to have work for you and tell why.

MESSAGE MESS-UP

Use the decoding dial to decode these "messed-up messages." Write a reply to each message.

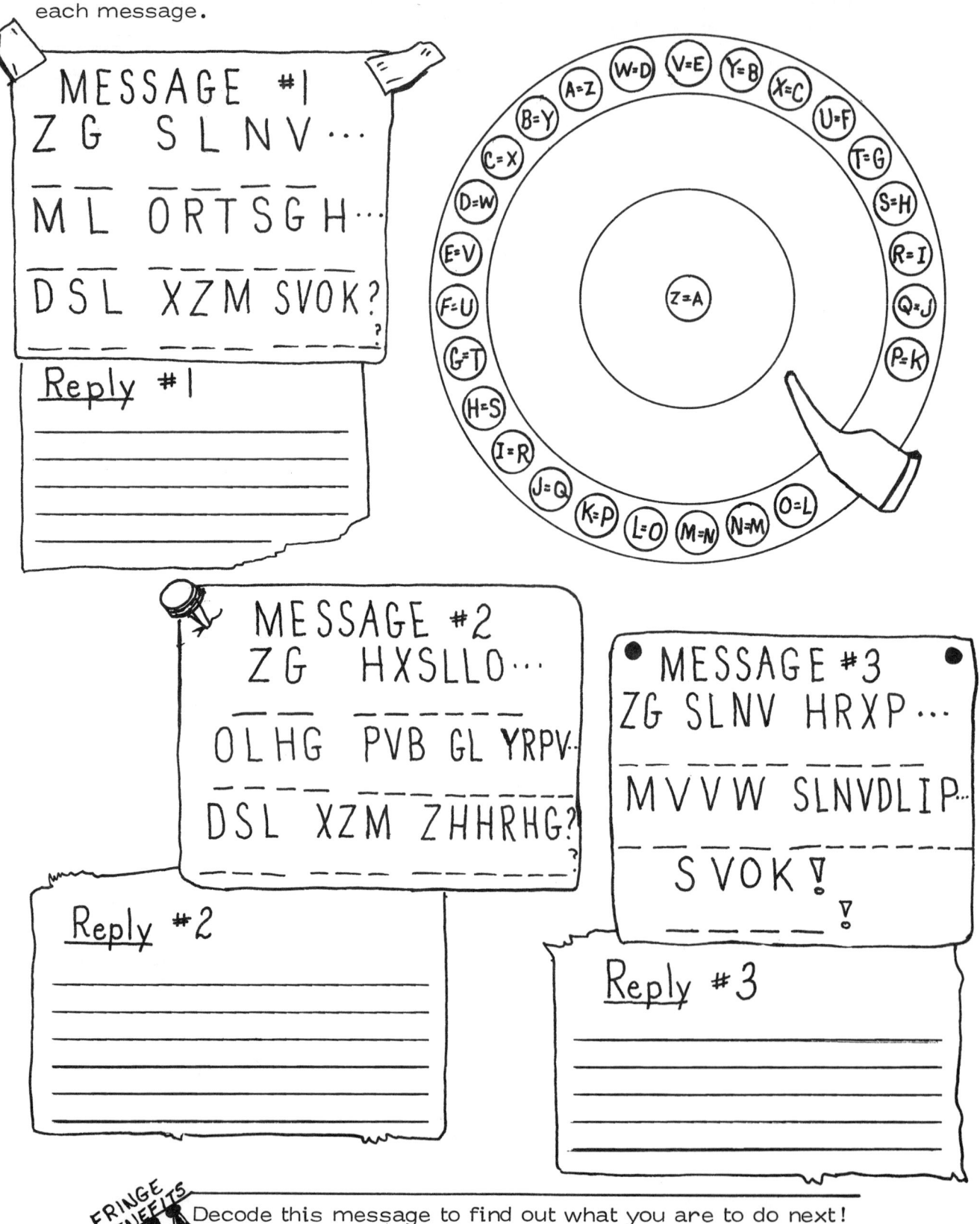

MESSAGE #1

ZG SLNV...
__ __ __ __ __ __

ML ORTSGH...
__ __ __ __ __ __ __ __

DSL XZM SVOK?
__ __ __ __ __ __ __ __ __ __ __?

Reply #1

MESSAGE #2

ZG HXSLLO...
__ __ __ __ __ __ __ __

OLHG PVB GL YRPV...
__ __ __ __ __ __ __ __ __ __ __ __ __

DSL XZM ZHHRHG?
__ __ __ __ __ __ __ __ __ __ __?

Reply #2

MESSAGE #3

ZG SLNV HRXP...
__ __ __ __ __ __ __ __ __

MVVW SLNVDLIP...
__ __ __ __ __ __ __ __ __ __ __ __

SVOK!
__ __ __ __!

Reply #3

Decode this message to find out what you are to do next!

XLWV   NVHHZTV   ULI   UIRVMW!!
__ __ __ __   __ __ __ __ __ __ __   __ __ __   __ __ __ __ __ __!!

72

MONETARY CONNECTIONS

Spending money is an important part of career interdependence. As you supply the information below, try to think of the many ways people are required to work together in daily life.

1. List four jobs for which people are paid a salary.
   _____ _____
   _____ _____

2. Give two examples of jobs involved in banking.
   _____ _____

3. Give two examples of places where people spend money on clothing.
   _____ _____

4. Name three types of services paid for in the home.
   _____ _____
   _____

5. Give two examples of ways people spend money for medical services.
   _____ _____

6. Give three ways people spend money on transportation.
   _____ _____
   _____

7. Name two types of insurance coverage people buy.
   _____ _____

8. Name three places where people spend money on food.
   _____ _____
   _____

9. Give two examples of how people spend money for education.
   _____ _____

10. Give three examples of people spending money for recreation.
    _____ _____
    _____

11. Name three ways in which you spend your money.
    _____ _____
    _____

IZZY IRRESPONSIBLE?

Read this story about a typical day in Izzy's life and answer the questions below.

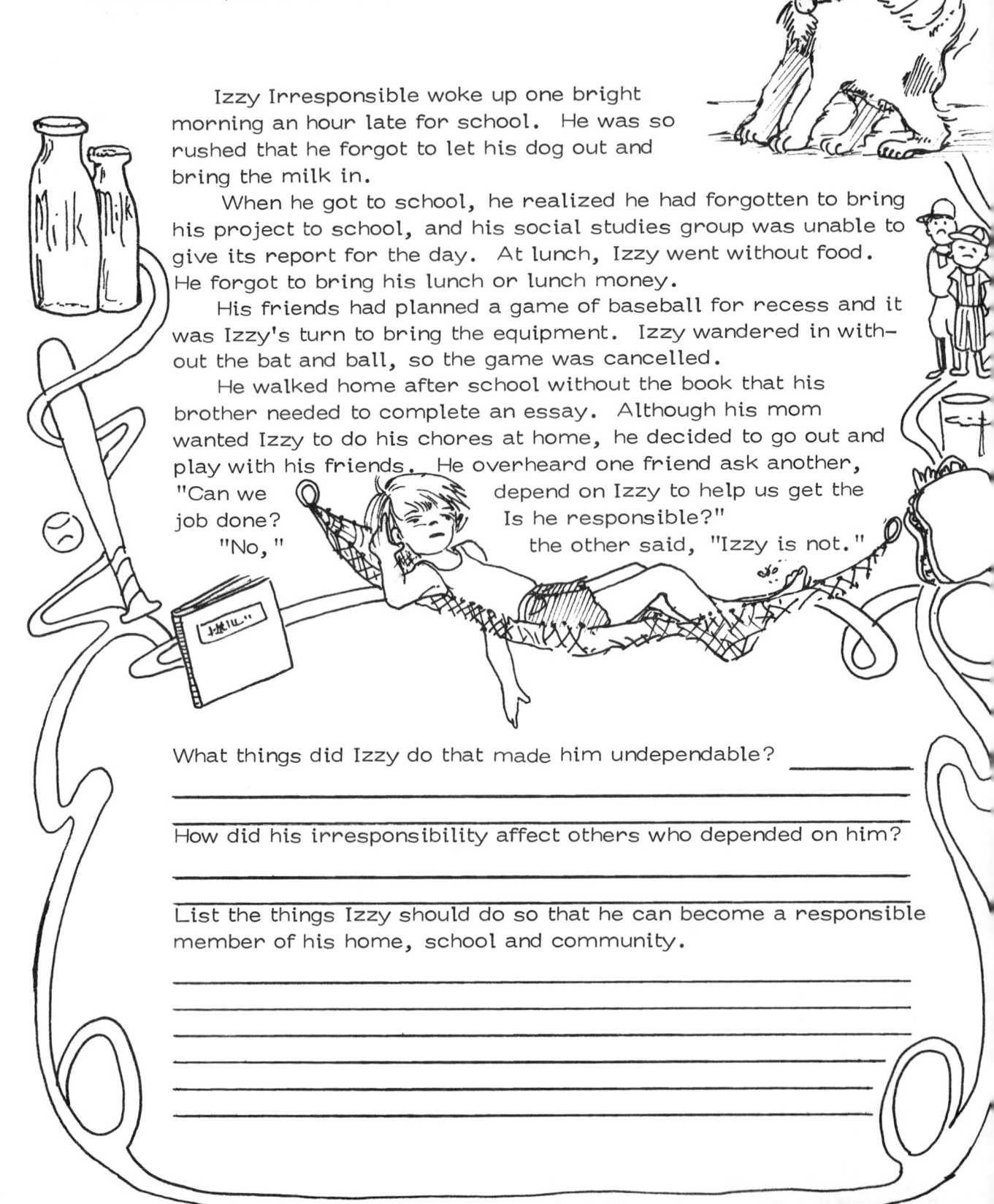

Izzy Irresponsible woke up one bright morning an hour late for school. He was so rushed that he forgot to let his dog out and bring the milk in.

When he got to school, he realized he had forgotten to bring his project to school, and his social studies group was unable to give its report for the day. At lunch, Izzy went without food. He forgot to bring his lunch or lunch money.

His friends had planned a game of baseball for recess and it was Izzy's turn to bring the equipment. Izzy wandered in without the bat and ball, so the game was cancelled.

He walked home after school without the book that his brother needed to complete an essay. Although his mom wanted Izzy to do his chores at home, he decided to go out and play with his friends. He overheard one friend ask another, "Can we depend on Izzy to help us get the job done? Is he responsible?"
"No," the other said, "Izzy is not."

What things did Izzy do that made him undependable? _____
_____
_____

How did his irresponsibility affect others who depended on him?
_____
_____

List the things Izzy should do so that he can become a responsible member of his home, school and community.
_____
_____
_____
_____
_____

NATURAL FORCES

Describe how these natural disaster situations require workers to plan and work together.

_____
_____
_____
_____
_____
_____

Forest Fire

Tornado

_____
_____
_____
_____

_____
_____
_____

Flood

Water Shortage

_____
_____
_____
_____

FRINGE BENEFITS Look in the newspaper for articles about emergency situations. Discuss the events and how the people helped one another.

75

LENDING LANDS

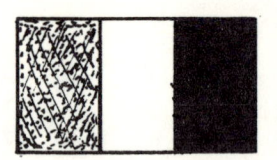

We depend on people from other countries for many things. Complete these statements about how people from all over the world contribute to our daily lives.

List three things you use in your home that were manufactured in foreign countries.

Item 1 _____ _____
(country)

Item 2 _____ _____
(country)

Item 3 _____ _____
(country)

List three things you enjoy eating that are native to other lands (example: tacos from Mexico).

_____ _____
(country)

_____ _____
(country)

_____ _____
(country)

Name three famous people from other countries who have influenced us.

Name _____ _____
(country)
Contribution _____

Name _____ _____
(country)
Contribution _____

Name _____ _____
(country)
Contribution _____

Draw a picture of ten things from our country on which people of other countries depend.

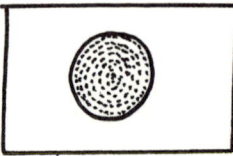

PUZZLE PARTS

Make the parts of this puzzle work by writing a paragraph about how people from different countries can help each other in the production of needed goods and services.

- Oil Country
- Auto Country
- Rubber Country
- Nuts and Bolts Country
- Glass Country

_____
_____
_____
_____
_____
_____
_____
_____

FRINGE BENEFITS Make a country puzzle of your own. Examples for puzzle topics are: clothing, medicine, food, radios and cameras. Use your imagination! Ask a classmate to tell how the pieces can work together.

WORLD WISE

Imagine that you are the "Ambassador of World Friendship." Your job is to help people from all lands to work together in love and harmony. Write what you as the Ambassador would say in response to these questions.

Why should all people work together? _____
_____

What will you do to help people understand each other better? _____
_____
_____

Do you think it is important for people to share their resources? _____ Why?
_____
_____

What will you do to make the world a better place? _____
_____
_____

What do you think children can do to help promote world peace? _____
_____

Why do you think it's important to understand the way other people think and live
_____
_____

FRINGE BENEFITS Write a story about what it would be like to live and work in a different country.

78

VALUE EVALUATION

Write what you would do in each of these situations.

Your neighbor asked you to come home right after school to help clean up the back yard. On your way home a friend tells you that if you deliver her papers you may use her mini-bike for two hours. What do you do?

During school the principal announced that someone has lost $20.00. During recess you find a twenty-dollar bill on the playground. What do you do?

You and a friend have volunteered to make puppets for the class play. The night before the play your friend calls and tells you he can't finish his. He asks you if you will complete his and give him credit for doing the work. What do you do?

After ball practice you find the kind of glove on the field you have wanted for a long time. You want to take it home with you. What do you do?

You and your friends are playing in the park and find a rowboat on the beach. Someone suggests that you take it out for a ride on the lake, but you don't know how to swim. What do you do?

BORDER BOUNDARIES

List three ways in which these neighboring countries are probably alike.

_____
_____
_____

List three ways in which the countries may be different.

_____
_____
_____

Give three examples of how neighboring countries can work together to produce goods and services needed by both countries.

_____
_____
_____

Write a paragraph telling why countries that are close neighbors must cooperate with one another. (What can happen when neighbors fail to cooperate?)

_____
_____
_____

FRINGE BENEFITS Look in an atlas and make a list of four sets of neighboring countries. Example: United States and Canada.

POSITION PLACE

Assign the most qualified candidate to each of the group leadership roles. Give reasons for your selection.

Candidates

I.M. A. Goody
Good Leader
Organized
Reliable

B. Nice
Friendly
Fair
Talkative

C. Figures
Trustworthy
Careful and Neat
Excellent in Math

B. Led
Listens to Others
Follows Others
Predictable

I.M. Neat
Good Listener
Nice Handwriter
Best Subject: English

M. Flippy
Careless
Irresponsible
Best Subject: Recess

Position	Major Responsibilities	Your Selection	Why
President	In charge of all meetings and makes sure all work is done.		
Vice President	In charge of committees and assists president.		
Secretary	In charge of all written materials and takes meeting minutes.		
Treasurer	In charge of all money and keeps account of funds		

NAME: _____

Your Candidate

FRINGE BENEFITS Nominate yourself for a position and list your qualifications.

DEPENDENCY FILE

Use personal information to complete these dependence information cards.

CLOTHES

For clothing I depend on:
1. _____ to _____
2. _____ to _____
3. _____ to _____

FOOD

For food I depend on:
1. _____ to _____
2. _____ to _____
3. _____ to _____

Illness

When I am sick I depend on:
1. _____ to _____
2. _____ to _____
3. _____ to _____

School

At school I depend on:
1. _____ to _____
2. _____ to _____
3. _____ to _____

Home

At home I depend on:
1. _____ to _____
2. _____ to _____
3. _____ to _____

Fringe Benefits: Make dependency cards for other needs. Examples: sports, transportation, hobbies, personal appearance, etc. For extra Fringe Benefits, make a card titled "Who depends on me?"

SCRAMBLED NEEDS

Unscramble the letters in each box to find who has the special need in the sentence. Complete each sentence by:

(1) writing the name of the person with the special need in the first blank
(2) writing the name of a person who can supply that need in the second blank

abby — I am a _____ and I depend on my _____ to change my diapers.

hcaco — I am a football _____ and I depend on the _____ to follow my game plan.

ctroa — I am an _____ and I depend on a _____ to supply my script for the play.

ookc — I am a _____ and I depend on a _____ to serve my food to customers.

ioptl — I am a _____ and I depend on a _____ to repair my airplane.

edtsnit — I am a _____ and I depend on a _____ to clean my patients' teeth.

utdnset — I am a _____ and I depend on a _____ to help me with my lessons.

cbtuhre — I am a _____ and I depend on a _____ to supply me with meat.

tinpeat — I am a _____ and I depend on the _____ to set my broken arm.

apnecrrte — I am a _____ and I depend on the _____ to supply me with lumber for my building.

iblarniar — I am a _____ and I depend on the _____ to take care of the borrowed book.

83

JOINT DECISIONS

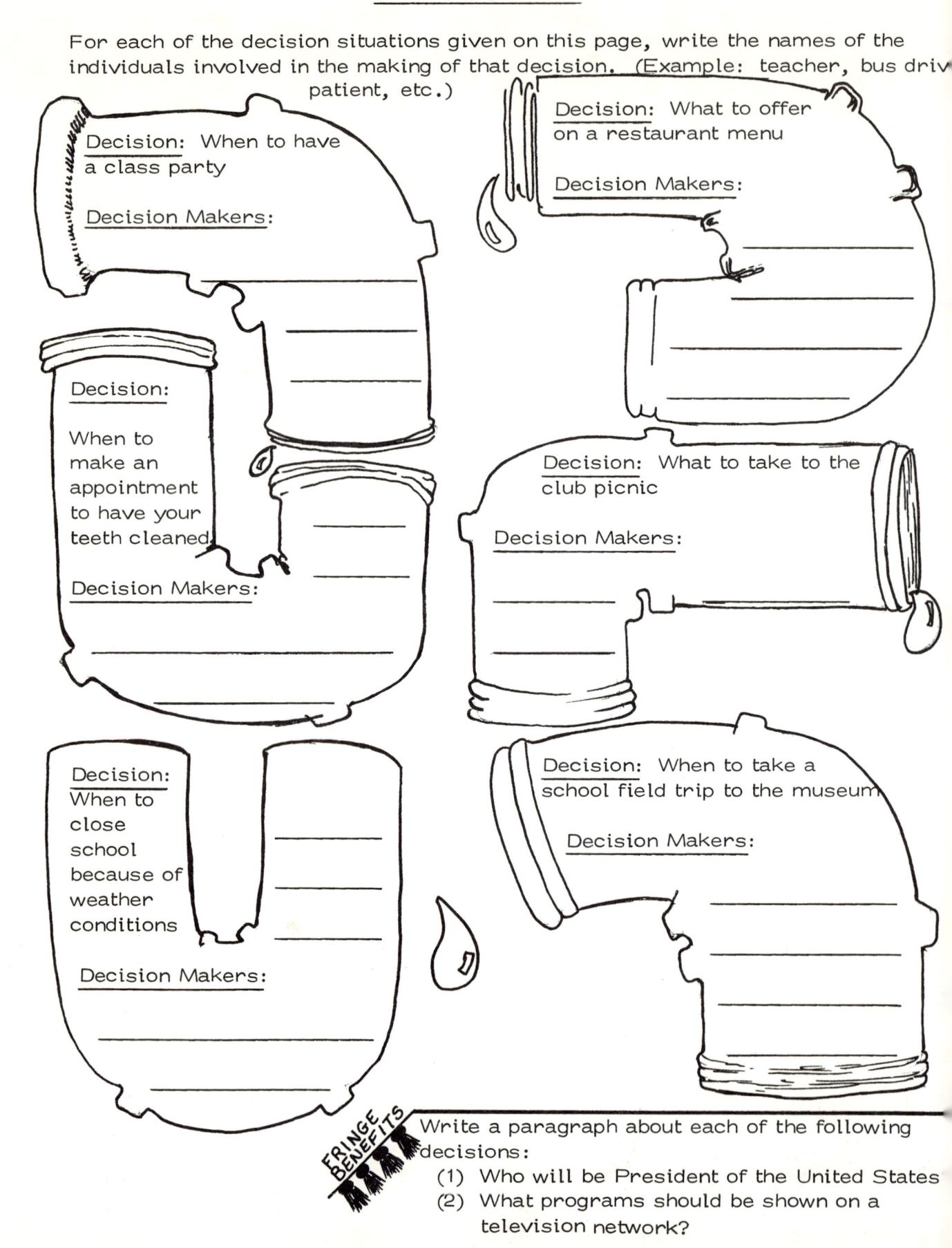

For each of the decision situations given on this page, write the names of the individuals involved in the making of that decision. (Example: teacher, bus driver, patient, etc.)

Decision: When to have a class party

Decision Makers: _____
_____
_____

Decision: What to offer on a restaurant menu

Decision Makers: _____
_____
_____

Decision: When to make an appointment to have your teeth cleaned

Decision Makers: _____
_____
_____

Decision: What to take to the club picnic

Decision Makers: _____
_____
_____

Decision: When to close school because of weather conditions

Decision Makers: _____
_____
_____

Decision: When to take a school field trip to the museum

Decision Makers: _____
_____
_____

FRINGE BENEFITS

Write a paragraph about each of the following decisions:
(1) Who will be President of the United States
(2) What programs should be shown on a television network?

84

looking to the future

NOTES

CAREER COAT OF ARMS

Draw a picture for each of the career areas in your Career Coat of Arms to match your career goals. Write a short sentence or phrase (a "motto") to describe your ideal career.

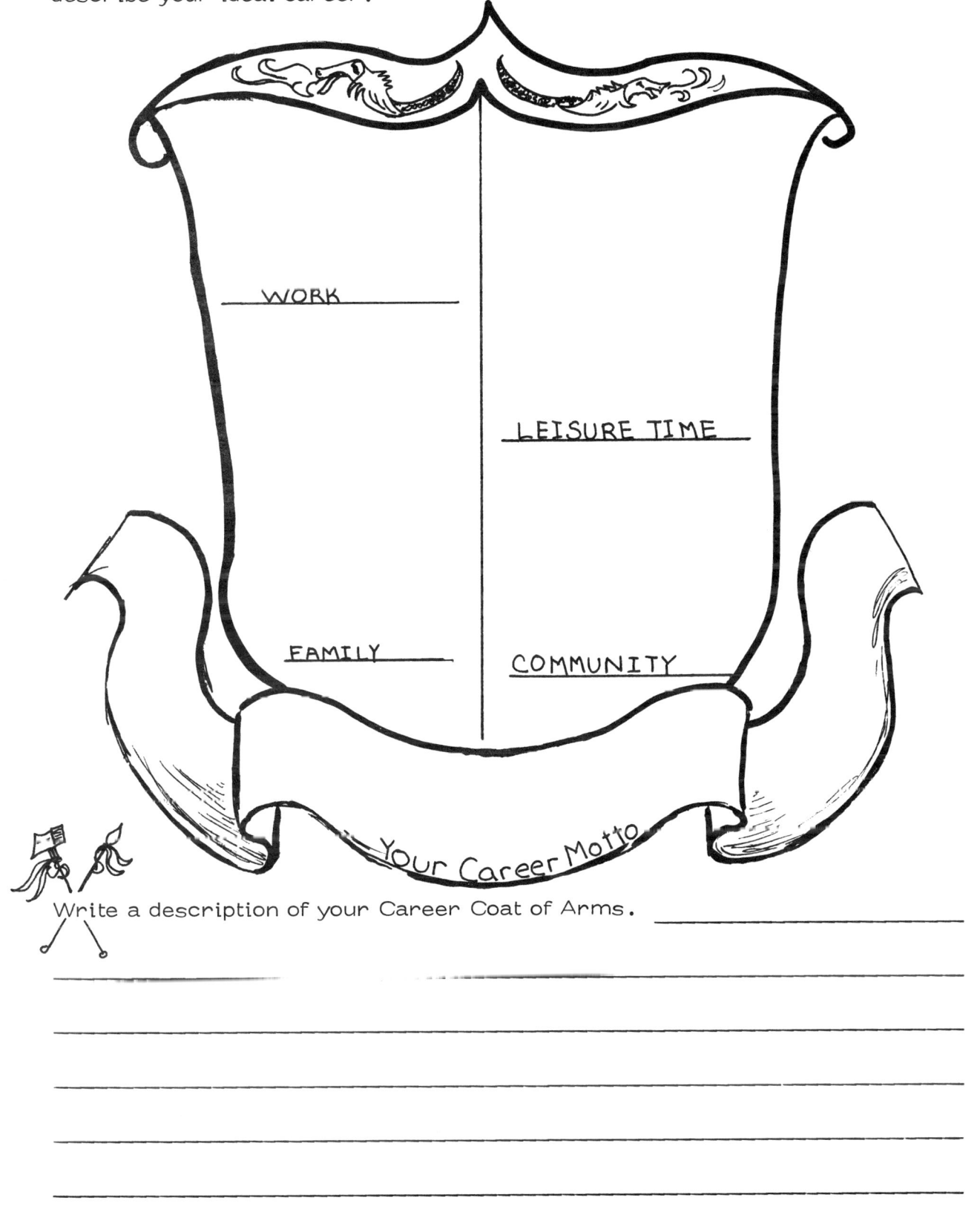

WORK

LEISURE TIME

FAMILY

COMMUNITY

Your Career Motto

Write a description of your Career Coat of Arms. _____

_____
_____
_____
_____
_____

GOAL TO GO

Define your career goal.
_____
_____

What education or training will you need to reach your career goal? Write the steps in the numbered spaces along the way up.

elementary school	graduate school	special school
secondary school		vocational school
college		on-the-job training

TERM MATCH

Below are words which often appear in help wanted ads. Using your dictionary, match each word with a definition.

Applicant	Money made by salesman on goods or services sold by him
Experience	Asking for the job
Retail	Working the full forty hours per week
Advancement	"Extra" benefits of the job
Salary	Working less than forty hours per week
Benefits	Money paid for work done
Fringe benefits	Exact times of work
Apply	Advantages of the job
References	Person doing the hiring
Graduate	Chance to get ahead in a job
Incentives	Business or company department concerned with hiring and record keeping of the workers
Personnel	Selling directly to the consumer
Employer	Reasons to want the job
Hours	Previous work experience (or previous jobs held)
Part-time	Person who has completed a course of study
Full-time	Person asking for the job
Commission	Sources (or letters) which confirm worker's previous experiences

Use the "Help Wanted" ads in the newspaper and find two words or terms of which you are unsure of the meaning. Write the words below and their definitions. Compare your words with those found by a friend.

_____

_____

See how many of the words given above you can find in the newspaper "Help Wanted" section and circle them.

IT'S ALL IN THE "NAME"

Describe your career goals by using the letters in your name. The careers may either begin or end with the letters in your first or last names.

For example: Mary chose these careers to describe her goals:

        M   eteorologist
        A   stronaut
        R   esearcher
 attorne Y

Your name and careers:

Write a paragraph explaining how the careers you have chosen best describe your career goals.

Describe how you plan to reach these goals.

FRINGE BENEFITS

90

INTERVIEW INQUIRY

Choose a job that is interesting to you. Prepare for the job interview by answering these sample interview questions. (Note: Write your answers as you would say them in an actual interview.)

Interviewer's Questions   Your Answers

1. "For which job are you applying?"

2. "What are your qualifications for this job?"

3. "What work experience do you have?"

4. "What hours can you work?"

5. "How much pay do you expect to receive?"

6. "Why do you want to work for this company?"

7. "What future career goals do you have?"

FRINGE BENEFITS Write six questions you would like to ask your potential employer during the interview.

YOUR OWN BAG

Choose a career that is interesting to you. Fill in the information needed to fill the career "bag."

Career: _____

Job Description:

Skills needed:

Education necessary:

Tools of the trade:

Dress for the occupation:

Job location:

FRINGE BENEFITS Make a scrapbook about your career. Use magazines to find pictures illustrating the job involved. Find "help wanted ads" for your desired job in the newspaper. Comp your career with those chosen by three classmates.

WORKING EXPERIENCES

Volunteer work is a good way to gain experience. Help these boys and girls by listing the jobs they might like to have in the future and places where they can find volunteer work to gain experience now.

Volunteer Work to Gain Experience

Mary likes animals. List some jobs she might like to have in the future.

_____
_____
_____
_____

_____
_____
_____
_____

Jim wants to work with young children. List some jobs he might like to have in the future.

_____
_____
_____
_____

_____
_____
_____
_____

Susan wants to work outdoors and close to nature. List some jobs she might like to have in the future.

_____
_____
_____
_____

_____
_____
_____
_____

Alex wants to help people solve their problems. List some jobs he might like to have in the future.

_____
_____
_____
_____

_____
_____
_____
_____

List your interests.

_____
_____
_____

_____
_____
_____

SIGN-N-SEAL

Select a job you would like to have. Use this stationary to write a letter requesting a friend to write a letter of personal reference to your prospective employer. In your note you will need to include:

(1) Request
(2) Type of job wanted
(3) Skills required
(4) Name and address of employer
(5) Date of requested completion

Date _____

Dear _____,

Sincerely,

CLOTHES CONTACT

Help Sue and Sam decide what to wear to their job interviews. Circle the clothes and accessories that are appropriate and put an "X" on the ones that are not appropriate.

SUE'S CLOSET

Sue should wear the clothes I have circled because _____
_____

SAM'S CLOSET

Sam should wear the clothes I have circled because _____
_____
_____

FRINGE BENEFITS Write a paragraph explaining why they should not wear the clothes you have marked with an "X."

95

APPLICATION BLANK

The following terms are often used on application forms. Briefly describe the information each term is requesting and then give the information asked for according to your own record.

Applicant: _____

Residence: _____

Height: _____

Weight: _____

Physical Defects: _____

Birthplace: _____

Date of Birth: _____

Citizenship: _____

Nationality: _____

Marital Status: _____

Maiden Name: _____

Dependents: _____

Selective Service Status: _____

Education: _____

LOOK INTO THE FUTURE

Match the following jobs which you might be performing now with their possible future careers. Draw a line from each "Now Job" to its "Future Career."

Now Job	Future Career
making candy	waiter
lawn care	zoo keeper
delivery person	decorator
house cleaning	auctioneer
caring for pets	researcher
selling magazines	baker
repairing toys	tailor
setting the table	gardener
caring for house plants	social worker
child care	postal worker
garage sales	custodian
making doll clothes	ecologist
library helper	mechanic
collecting paper for recycling	florist
painting	store clerk

Choose one job which you do now. Create an advertisement for your "Now Job" and one for its possible "Future Career." Use magazines, newspaper advertisements or the yellow pages of the telephone directory for ideas.

WORK WANTED

Write a Work Wanted ad for the newspaper for a summer job you would like to have. Some suggested jobs are babysitting, dog-sitting, lawn care, tutoring, housecleaning, etc. Use your newspaper as a resource for other ideas.

Classified Ads

June 2, 1979

D-7 section 5

Work Wanted

FRINGE BENEFITS: Write a Work Wanted ad for a job you would like to have in the future.

NOW AND THEN

Select a job you would like to have. Describe the job as it is now. Then look into the future and describe what you think it will be like when you enter the job market.

Job Title _____   Job Title _____

Description _____   Description _____
_____   _____

Duties _____   Duties _____
_____   _____

Tools of the trade _____   Tools of the trade _____
_____   _____
_____   _____

Place of business _____   Place of business _____
_____   _____

Skills and education needed ____   Skills and education needed ____
_____   _____
_____   _____

Pay and fringe benefits   Pay and fringe benefits
(vacations, working times)   (vacations, working times)
_____   _____
_____   _____

Opportunities for advancement   Opportunities for advancement
_____   _____
_____   _____

List the major changes you have predicted.
List the new skills you will need to perform your job.

CAREER WHEELS

The skills you are learning in school are related to success in many occupations. Complete these career wheels by writing the jobs on the spokes of the wheels associated with the subjects on the wheel hubs. Note: An example for each has been given.

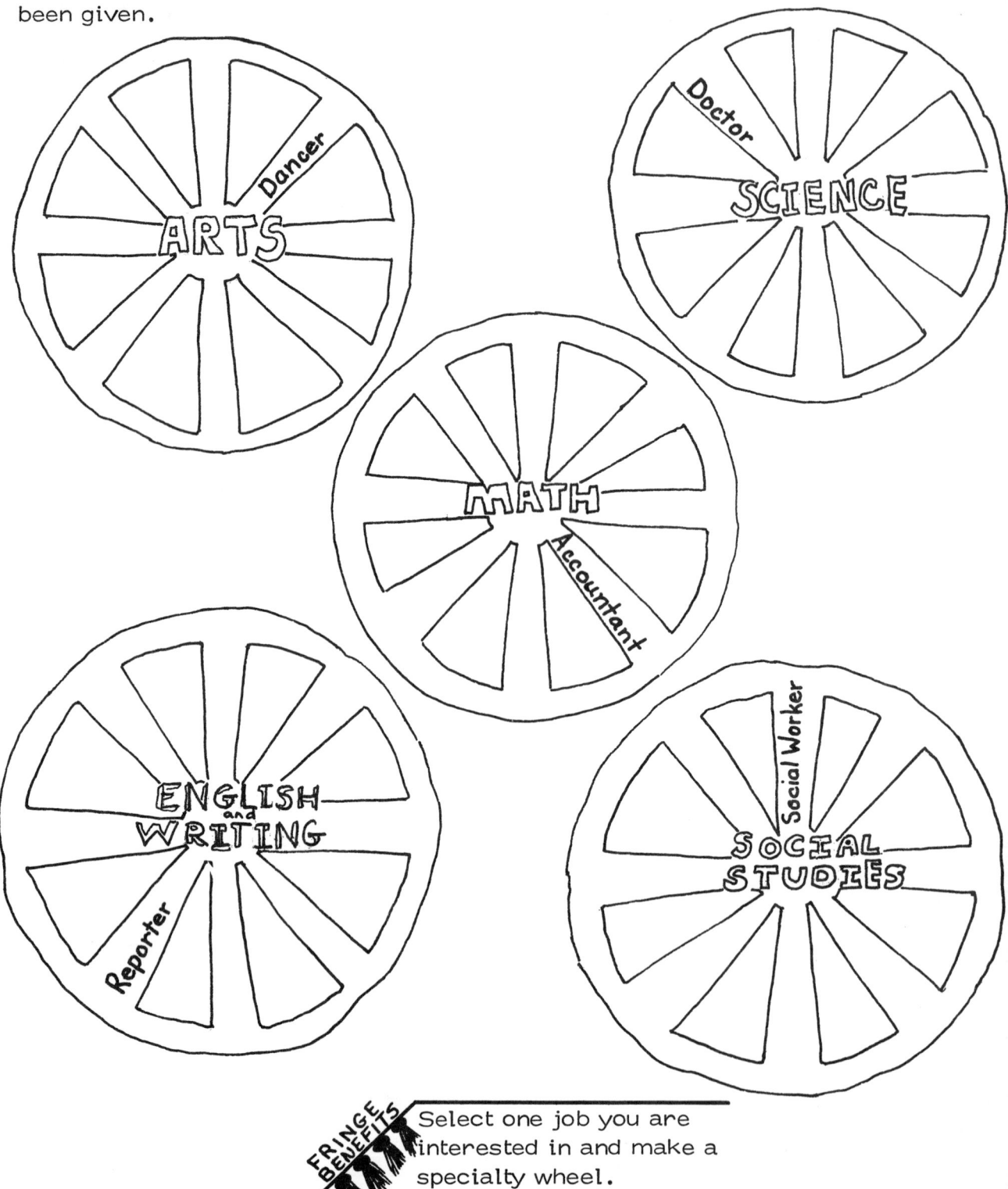

ARTS — Dancer

SCIENCE — Doctor

MATH — Accountant

ENGLISH and WRITING — Reporter

SOCIAL STUDIES — Social Worker

FRINGE BENEFITS: Select one job you are interested in and make a specialty wheel.

FUTURE I.D.

"IMAGINE"

You are 25 years old. Complete this personal computer resume to describe yourself.

DATA:

Name _____ Date _____

Age _____ Birthdate _____

Home Address _____ Occupation _____

_____ Business Address _____

_____ _____

Telephone _____

Personal Description: Job Description:

Hair _____ _____

Eyes _____ _____

Height _____ _____

Weight _____ Salary _____

Educational Background: _____

Hobbies, Interests, Leisure Time Activities: _____

Personal Statement (Briefly describe how you got where you are and how you plan to get where you want to go.):

ELEVATION EXPLORATION

Explore a career of your choice by writing in the information suggested by the title of each floor of this career office building.

PENT HOUSE

Floor 5: Career Future Outlook

Floor 4: Promotions and Opportunities / Finances

Floor 3: Benefits

Floor 2: Qualifications

Floor 1: Job Description

TIME SPAN

An important part of any job is scheduling time--knowing when to do what chore. For practice in future job competency, answer the following questions:

1. List ten things you must do today. (Examples: getting dressed, going to school, doing math homework, meeting team for practice, doing home chores, etc.) Give the time that they are to be done.

   Activity   Time

   1. _____   _____
   2. _____   _____
   3. _____   _____
   4. _____   _____
   5. _____   _____
   6. _____   _____
   7. _____   _____
   8. _____   _____
   9. _____   _____
   10. _____   _____

2. Plan for the future. List five activities (other than those above) which you must complete tomorrow. Give the time they must be completed and how long you think each activity will require.

   1. _____   _____   _____
   2. _____   _____   _____
   3. _____   _____   _____
   4. _____   _____   _____
   5. _____   _____   _____

FRINGE BENEFITS

(1) Compare your lists with those of a friend. How do the activities differ? How are they alike? Did you both need the same amount of time for like activities?

(2) Make a time schedule for important activities of the week.

AT YOUR SERVICE

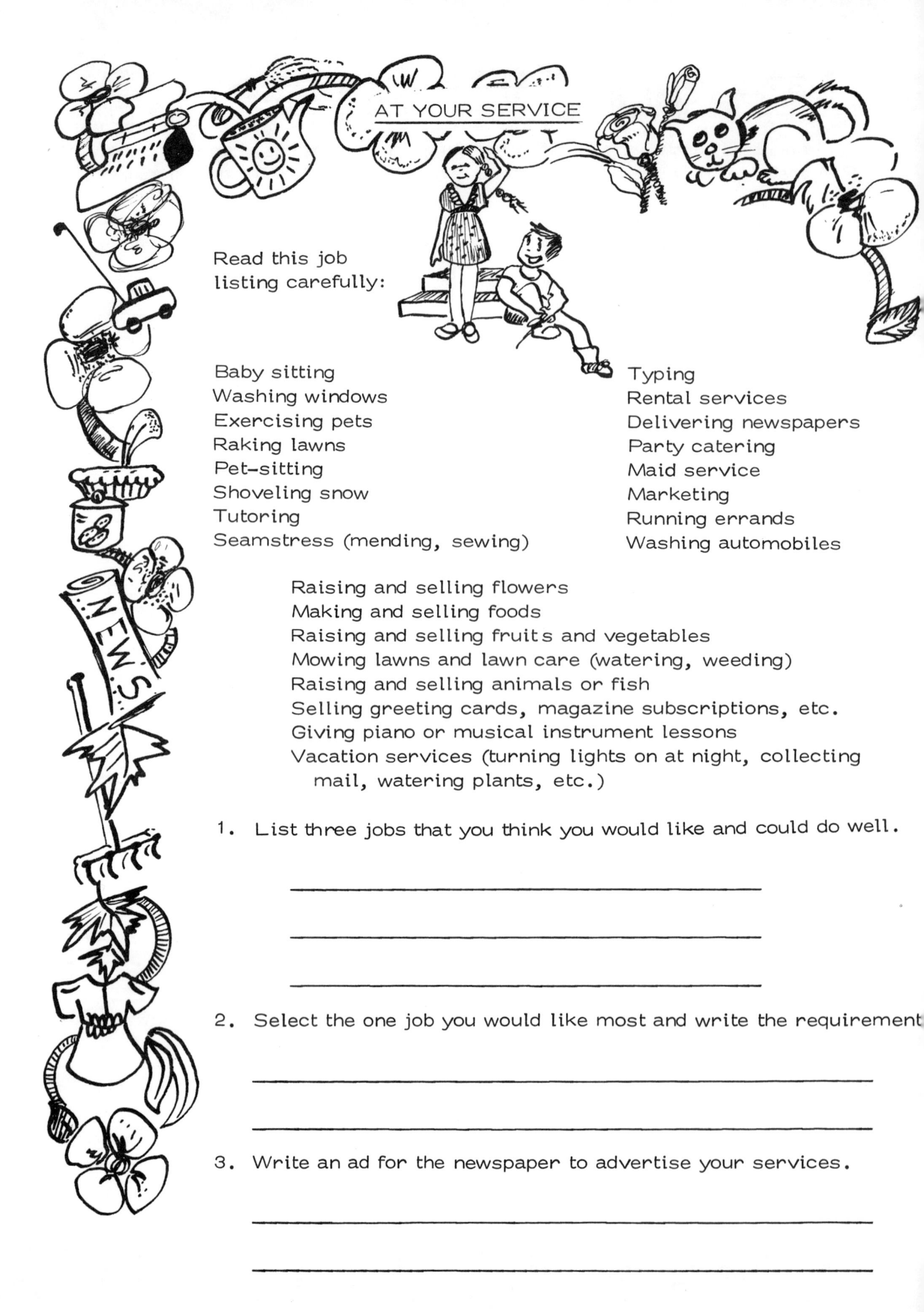

Read this job listing carefully:

Baby sitting
Washing windows
Exercising pets
Raking lawns
Pet-sitting
Shoveling snow
Tutoring
Seamstress (mending, sewing)

Typing
Rental services
Delivering newspapers
Party catering
Maid service
Marketing
Running errands
Washing automobiles

Raising and selling flowers
Making and selling foods
Raising and selling fruits and vegetables
Mowing lawns and lawn care (watering, weeding)
Raising and selling animals or fish
Selling greeting cards, magazine subscriptions, etc.
Giving piano or musical instrument lessons
Vacation services (turning lights on at night, collecting mail, watering plants, etc.)

1. List three jobs that you think you would like and could do well.

   _____

   _____

   _____

2. Select the one job you would like most and write the requirement

   _____

   _____

3. Write an ad for the newspaper to advertise your services.

   _____

   _____

SELECTED REFERENCES

Student References

Ancona, George. And What Do You Do? New York: E. P. Dutton & Co., Inc., 1976.

Arnold, Walter M. (ed.). Career Opportunities for Technicians & Specialists. Chicago: J. G. Ferguson Publishing Co., 1969.

Benson, Christopher. Careers in Animal Care. Minneapolis: Lerner Publications Co., 1974.

Berger, Gilda. Jobs That Help the Consumer and Homemaker. New York: Lothrop, Lee & Shepard Co., 1974.

Brunetti, Cledo and Clifford Higgerson. Your Future in a Changing World. New York: Richards Rosen Press, Inc., 1970.

Cashin, James A. Careers & Opportunities in Accounting. New York: E. P. Dutton & Co., Inc., 1965.

Davis, Mary Lee. Careers in a Bank. Minneapolis: Lerner Publications Co., 1973.

Davis, Mary. Careers in a Medical Center. Minneapolis: Lerner Publications Co., 1973.

Davis, Mary Lee. Careers in Printing. Minneapolis: Lerner Publications Co., 1973.

Dean, Jennifer Brooks. Careers in a Department Store. Minneapolis: Lerner Publications Co., 1973.

Dietz, Betty Warner. You Can Work in the Communications Industry. New York: The John Day Company, 1970.

Englebardt, Stanley L. Jobs in Health Care. New York: Lothrop, Lee & Shepard Co., 1973.

Evans, J. A. I Know A Telephone Operator. New York: G. P. Putnam's Sons, 1971.

Evers, Dora R. and S. Norman Feingold. Your Future in Exotic Occupations. New York: Rosen Press, 1972.

Fenten, D. X. *Ms. - M.D.* Philadelphia: The Westminster Press, 1974.

Graham, Ada and Frank Graham, Jr. *The Great American Shopping Cart.* New York: Simon and Schuster, 1969.

Halacy, D. S., Jr. *Survival in the World of Work.* New York: Charles Scribner's Sons, 1975.

Heine, Robert. *Your Future in Traffic Management.* New York: Richards Rosen Press, Inc., 1967.

Johnson, George. *Your Career in Advertising.* New York: Julian Messner, 1966.

Kay, Eleanor. *Health Care Ideas.* New York: Franklin Watts, 1973.

Klever, Anita. *Women in Television.* Philadelphia: The Westminster Press, 1975.

Lee, Essie E., *Careers in the Health Field.* New York: Julian Messner, 1972.

McGonagle, Bob and Marquita McGonagle. *Careers in Sports.* New York: Lothrop, Lee & Shepard Co., 1975.

McLeod, Sterling. *Careers in Consumer Protection.* New York: Julian Messner, 1974.

Mitchell, Joyce Slayton. *Free To Choose.* New York: Delacorte Press, 1976.

Mitchell, Joyce Slayton. *Other Choices For Becoming A Woman.* New York: Delacorte Press, 1976.

Ray, Jo Anne. *Careers With a Police Department.* Minneapolis: Lerner Publications Co., 1973.

Rider, John R. *Your Future in Broadcasting.* New York: Richard Rosen Press, 1971.

Seed, Suzanne. *Saturday's Child.* Chicago: J. Philip O'Hara, Inc., 1973.

Shay, Arthur. *What It's Like To Be A Teacher.* Chicago: Reilly & Lee Books, 1971.

Splaver, Sarah. Non-traditional Careers For Women. New York: Julian Messner, 1973.

Splaver, Sarah. Paraprofessions - Careers of the Future and the Present. New York: Julian Messner, 1973.

Tannenbaum, Beulah and Myra Stillman. Feeding The City. New York: McGraw-Hill, 1971.

Wakin, Edward. Jobs in Communications. New York: Lothrop, Lee & Shepard Co., 1974.

Teacher References

Calhoun, Calfrey and Alton Finch. Vocational & Career Education: Concepts & Operations. Belmont, California: Wadsworth Publishing Co., Inc., 1976.

Career Education: A Handbook for Implementation. Washington, D. C.: U. S. Government Printing Office, 1972.

Ferguson, J. G. Career Opportunities. Chicago: J. G. Ferguson Publishing Co., 1971.

Fraenkel, William A. How To Get A Job - A Handy Guide for Jobseekers. Washington, D. C.: The President's Committee on Employment of the Handicapped, 1966.

Gibson, Robert Leone. Career Development in the Elementary School. Columbus, Ohio: Robert L. Gibson, Merrill Series, 1972.

Goldhammer, Keith and Robert E. Taylor. Career Education: Perspective and Promise. Columbus, Ohio: Charles E. Merrill Publishing Co., 1972.

Hodgson, J. E. Handbook for Analyzing Jobs. Washington, D. C.: U. S. Department of Labor, U. S. Government Printing Office, 1972.

Hoyt, Kenneth. Career Education and the Elementary School Teacher. Salt Lake City: Olympus Publishing Co., 1973.

Hoyt, Kenneth B. and Jean R. Hebeler (eds.). Career Education for Gifted and Talented Students. Salt Lake City: Olympus Publishing Co., 1974.

Hoyt, Kenneth. *Career Education: What It Is & How To Do It*. Salt Lake City: Olympus Publishing Co., 1974.

Kenneke, Larry, Dennis C. Nystrom and Ronald W. Stadt. *Planning & Organizing Career Curricula: Articulated Edition*. Indianapolis: Howard W. Sams & Co., Inc., 1973.

Lovejoy, Clarence Earle. *Career & Vocational School Guide*. 4th ed. New York: Simon & Schuster, 1973.

Mangum, Garth, Jemes Becker, Garn Coombs and Patricia Marshall (eds.). *Career Education in the Academic Classroom*. Salt Lake City: Olympus Publishing Co., 1975.

Occupational Outlook Handbook. Washington, D. C.: U. S. Government Printing Office, 1972-73.

Wigglesworth, David C. *Career Education - A Reader*. San Francisco: Canfield Press, 1975.

Testing & Screening Instruments

California Test of Personality, Louis Thorpe, Willis Clark and Ernest Tiegs. California Test Bureau (Grades K - Adult).

Devereux Child Behavior Rating Scale, George Spivak and Jules Spotts. Devereux Foundation Press (Ages 8 - 12).

Devereux Elementary School Behavior Rating Scale, George Spivak and Marshall Swift. Devereux Foundation Press (Grades K - 6)

The Vineland Social Maturity Scale, Edgar A. Doll. American Guidance Service, Inc.

Walker Problem Behavior Identification Checklist, Hill M. Walker. Western Psychological Services (Grades 4 - 6).